For Melek-Mary and Eric

365 STORY BIBLE

By Meg Wang

Illustrated By Heather Stuart

Contents

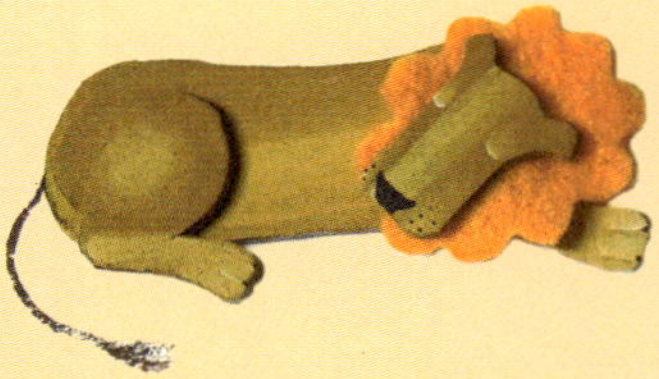

The New Testament

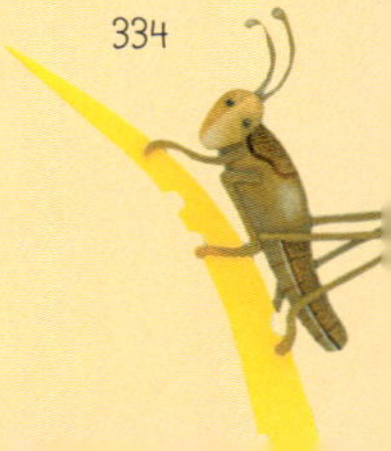

The Old

Testament

1

God makes light

Genesis 1:1-5

In the beginning, there was no earth or sky
or animals or people. Everything was quiet and dark.
Then God said, "Let there be light!" A beautiful
warm glow filled the darkness. "That's good!"
God said to himself, and he called the light "day"
and the darkness "night".

2

God makes sky

Genesis 1:6-8

Then God said, "Wouldn't it be great to have a wide beautiful space?" So he made a big, blue, heavenly sky above the waters below. He stood back to look at what he had made. "I'll call this 'sky'," God said.

3

God makes plants and trees

Genesis 1:9-13

God gathered the water together in some places, revealing dry land. He called the land "earth" and the water "seas". "This is great!" God said. "But it needs something else." God then filled the earth with plants and trees and fruit and flowers and even... vegetables.

4

God makes the sun, moon and stars

Genesis 1:14-19

God arranged lights in the sky to separate the day and the night. The beautiful fiery sun gave light during the day and a cool bright moon with sparkly stars lightened up the dark night sky.

5

God makes fish and birds

Genesis 1:20-23

God filled the seas with all kinds of creatures. Some crawled along the sea bed or clung to other creatures. Others had fins and tails and darted or swam or jumped through the waters. God filled the skies with winged birds that called and cooed and chattered and tweeted.

6

God makes animals

Genesis 1:24-25

Then God filled his world with animals: large and small, striped and patterned, smooth and furry. Some lived on the ground and others climbed trees. Now God's world was green and sunny and full of the sound of birds and animals. God was pleased with all he had made.

7
God makes man and woman

Genesis 1:26-31

God's world was amazing! But God still felt something was missing. So he made people – a man and a woman – to be his friends and look after all of his creatures, from the fish in the sea to the birds in the sky to every creepy crawly thing that lived on the earth.

8

God rests

Genesis 2:1-3

Imagine making the heavens and the earth and all the living creatures, big and small, not to mention all the different colors and patterns. That's a lot of work! God looked at everything he had made. It was not only good, it was very good. So God took a well-deserved rest.

9

The garden of Eden

Genesis 2:8-17

God made the garden of Eden with everything Adam and Eve needed – a clear stream with cool water to drink and trees full of delicious fruits. God told Adam and Eve they could eat from any tree except from one in the middle of the garden.

10

The sneaky serpent

Genesis 2:1-5

One day, a serpent came to tempt Eve. "Did God tell you not to eat from the tree in the middle of the garden? God knows if you eat from this tree, you will become as clever as he is. Try it and see..."

11

The first sin

Genesis 2:6-13

Eve looked at the beautiful, ripe fruit. She picked a piece and took a bite. Then she shared some with Adam, and he took a bite. When God called to them, they were ashamed and hid from him. They knew they had disobeyed him. They couldn't be God's friends any more.

12

Adam and Eve's punishment

Genesis 2:14-24

God made the serpent crawl on his belly for tricking Eve. God warned Eve she would feel pain when she had children. God told Adam he would have to work hard to grow food for his family. One day they would die. Everything had gone wrong because they would not trust God. Then God sent them away from the garden.

13

Cain and Abel

Genesis 4:1-2

After a while Adam and Eve had children, two sons. Cain was the older brother, and he worked in the fields growing food. Abel was the younger brother, who looked after the flocks of sheep and goats.

14

Gifts for God

Genesis 4:3-4

Cain and Abel wanted to give gifts to God to thank him for the good harvests and new-born animals. Abel chose his best lamb. Cain gave some of his grain. God was pleased with Abel's gift. But he saw what Cain was like inside. He knew Cain didn't really care about God.

15
Cain kills his brother

Genesis 4:5-8

Cain was angry. He sulked. God warned him to keep his bad temper under control. But instead of trying harder to please God, Cain became more angry and jealous of his brother. He asked Abel to go for a walk in the field. Then Cain attacked Abel – and killed him. "It's not my fault," Cain said. But God knew that it was.

16

Noah the good man

Genesis 6:5-10

As time went on, God saw that the world had become a terrible place. People told lies and cheated. They killed each other. God was sorry that he had ever made people to be his friends. He decided to start again. There was just one good man left. His name was Noah.

17

God's plan

Genesis 6:14-16

God told Noah that he would send a flood to destroy everything on earth. He wanted Noah to build a huge boat, an ark, so he could save his family and enough creatures to start a new world. The ark would be huge – longer than a football field and higher than a three-storey building!

18

Noah builds the ark

Genesis 6:22

Noah was very old. But he listened to God, and he trusted God. His neighbors probably thought he was crazy. Even his family thought he was crazy! But Noah sawed and hammered and worked hard building the ark, just as God had told him to, until one day, it was ready.

19
Two by two

Genesis 7:2-5

God then asked Noah to find two of every kind of animal – a male and a female – and put them on the ark. Clip-clop, clip-clop, shuffle-shuffle, paw-paw, flap-flap, tip-toe, tip-toe. The animals climbed on board, two-by-two, until Noah had gathered all the different kinds of creatures on the earth.

20

The flood

Genesis 7:11-12

The rain fell, day after day. Patter, patter, drip, drip, drip. Inside the ark, the animals stamped or plodded, wriggled or waddled or snoozed. Noah and Mrs Noah fed them and cleaned up after them and wondered when the rain would stop raining.

21

The raven

Genesis 8:6-7

Ssshh. Listen! No more rain. Noah watched and waited and waited a little longer... Then one day he set free a raven to see if it was time to leave the ark. The raven opened its wings and flew away. But it did not return to the ark.

22

The dove

Genesis 8:8-11

Then Noah sent out a dove. She flapped gently though the blue sky, looking for a place to rest her feet. When she finally returned to Noah, she was carrying a fresh green olive leaf! Noah knew that the water had gone down. Trees were growing again!

23
Leaving the ark

Genesis 8:15-22

Was it time to leave the ark? When God told Noah to open up the door, all the animals returned to the clean, fresh world God was giving to them. Noah thanked God for telling him how to build the ark and for keeping them safe from the flood waters.

24

The rainbow

Genesis 9:8-17

Noah looked up in the sky, and through the clouds, God had made a beautiful rainbow appear. God was very happy with Noah. "I will never destroy the earth by flood again," God said. "Whenever you see this rainbow, remember that I have promised you this."

25
God chooses Abraham

Genesis 12:1-4

A long time after Noah, God spoke to a man named Abraham. "It's time to move on," God said. "Pack up all your things and I will tell you where to go." Abraham and his wife Sarah were already old. They didn't know where they were going, but they trusted God.

26

Abraham moves to Canaan

Genesis 12:5

Abraham had lots of sheep and cattle. He gathered up the tents where he lived, and went with his wife, Sarah, his nephew, Lot, his servants and all of his animals...away from his home and across the hot, dusty desert. God led him to his new home, in Canaan.

A very special blessing

Genesis 12:7

The land was made green by water. It was a good place to be. "Now I will bless you, Abraham," God said. "This land will belong to your children and your children's children." But Abraham wondered how that could happen, when they didn't have even one tiny baby.

28

Not enough room!

Genesis 13:5-9

Abraham's sheep had baby sheep. His goats had baby goats. God blessed both Abraham and Lot so much that they couldn't move for animals! "Choose anywhere you would like to live," Abraham told Lot. "We'll share the land between us so there is room for us all to be happy."

29

Lot moves away

Genesis 13:10-13

Lot chose the land to the east, a beautiful green valley, watered by the River Jordan. He made his home near a place called Sodom, near another city called Gomorrah. But Lot did not have good neighbors. Both these places were full of bad people who did cruel things. Abraham stayed in Canaan.

30

Abraham welcomes strangers

Genesis 18:1-10

What was this? Three men walking in the desert? Abraham offered them somewhere to rest and made them a good meal. Soon he realized that God had sent them. "Get ready for a wonderful surprise," they said. "Sarah will have a baby this time next year!"

31

One good man

Genesis 18:17-33

God saw the bad things that happened in Sodom and Gomorrah and planned to destroy the cities. Abraham knew that God was good. So he asked, "Will you spare the cities if only ten good people live there?" God said, "I will spare them."

32

Sodom and Gomorrah

Genesis 19:1-13

God sent two angels to see if there were any good people in Sodom and Gomorrah. Lot was there. He welcomed them at the gate of the city, and invited the angels to his home. But the bad people there hammered on the door and tried to break in.

33

Lot's escape

Genesis 19:14-25

Lot tried to protect the angels. Lot was a good man. But the angels warned him to take his family and get away as quickly as he could. "Run for your lives – and don't look back!" they said. So Lot, Mrs Lot and their two daughters ran from the city.

34

The pillar of salt

Genesis 19:26

When Lot and his family were far from the city, fire and brimstone rained down on Sodom and Gomorrah. Everything there was destroyed. Lot and his daughters were safe but Mrs Lot forgot the warning the angels gave her. She looked back – and was turned into a pillar of salt.

35

Sarah's baby boy

Genesis 21:1-8

What was happening to Sarah? Her tummy was growing bigger and bigger! It was a miracle. "God has made me so happy!" said Sarah. Abraham smiled. He had trusted God and God had kept his promise. Abraham and Sarah soon had a little boy named Isaac.

36

A hard test for Abraham

Genesis 22:1-8

Sometimes you say, "I love you. I trust you. I'll do anything for you!" But do you really mean it? Abraham said he loved and trusted God. So when God asked Abraham to give back to him the little boy he loved so much, what did Abraham do?

37

Abraham's choice

Genesis 22:9-12

Abraham trusted God. He took Isaac to a special place. "We're going to show God how much we love him," Abraham told his son. And Isaac trusted his father, even when he saw the knife in his hand. Then, "Stop!" said an angel. Abraham put down the knife and hugged his son very, very tightly.

38
The ram

Genesis 22:13-18

Abraham saw a ram caught in a bush nearby. "Thank you, God, for letting me give you this ram instead of Isaac," he said. Then God spoke to Abraham. "I know you love me. I know you trust me. Because you obeyed me even when it was really hard, I will bless you, now and always."

39

The servant's prayer

Genesis 24:1-14

Abraham wanted to choose a wife for Isaac from his own people. So he sent his servant on a journey to find the right young woman for his grown up son.
"Help me to choose a good, kind woman," he prayed, "a girl who would offer me water to drink – and water all my ten camels too!"

40

Isaac's new wife

Genesis 24:15-27

A beautiful girl came to the well for water. "May I have a drink?" the servant asked her. "Of course!" she answered. Then the girl said, "Let me also bring water for your camels. They must be so thirsty!" The servant smiled. He knew that God had answered his prayer.

41

Abraham's grandsons

Genesis 25:20-25

Rebecca was the name of the beautiful girl. Isaac married her and Abraham was happy. When Rebecca felt the kicking of babies growing inside her, God told her that one day her twin sons would lead two separate nations, but that the older boy would serve the younger.

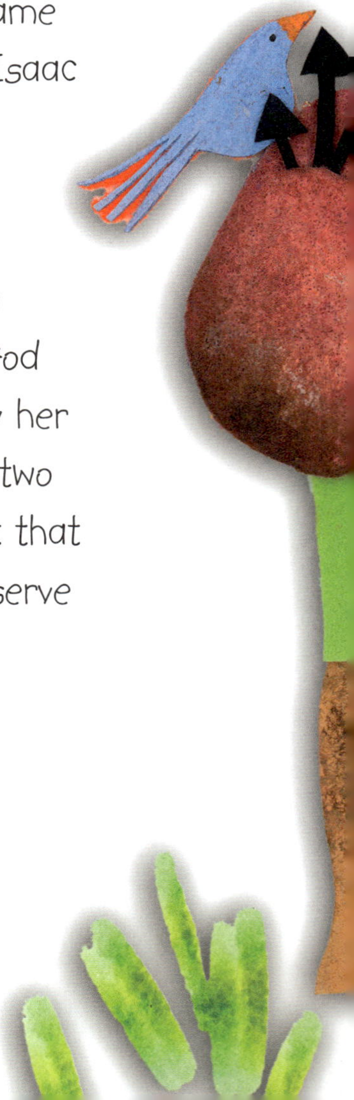

42
Esau the hunter

Genesis 25:26-28

Esau was born first. Even as a baby, he was already strong and hairy! He grew up to be a skillful hunter and he loved being outside. His father was proud of him. Isaac enjoyed spending time with Esau, looking after their many sheep and goats.

43

Jacob stays at home

Genesis 25:26-29

Jacob came second, but he was born holding on to Esau's heel. He didn't want to be overlooked or forgotten! Jacob grew up to be a peaceful boy. He preferred to spend time with his mother and was Rebecca's favorite. Esau would often come back from hunting to find Jacob cooking delicious food.

44

Tasty lentil stew!

Genesis 25:29-34

Esau flopped down. "I'm so hungry, I could die!" he told Jacob. "I'll give you some of this stew," said Jacob, "if you let me have father's blessing in your place!" "Anything!" replied Esau. So Esau sold his birthright to Jacob.

45
Isaac's last wish

Genesis 27:1-4

When Isaac became an old man, he couldn't see very well. One day he said to Esau, "My son, I know I am going to die soon. Please take your bow and arrow and hunt for me. Make me my favorite meal. Then I will give you my blessing as my oldest son."

46

Rebecca's plan

Genesis 27:5-17

Rebecca had another idea. She wanted Jacob to have the blessing instead. So while Esau was out hunting, she made Isaac's favorite meal. She then gave Jacob Esau's clothes to wear and covered him in goatskins so he could pretend to be his smelly, hairy brother!

47

Isaac blesses Jacob

Genesis 27:18-29

"Is that really you, Esau?" Isaac smelled the clothes Jacob wore and touched the furry skin covering his arms and neck. Then Isaac ate the meal Rebecca had made and blessed Jacob. "May God bless you always. You will become a rich man and will rule over your brother."

48
Jacob runs away

Genesis 27:30-46

When Esau found out what Jacob had done, he was very angry! "I'm going to kill my little brother for this! Please bless me too, father!" But Isaac told him it was too late ... Meanwhile, Rebecca sent Jacob away to stay with Laban, her brother, so that Esau couldn't hurt him!

49

Jacob dreams of angels

Genesis 28:10-22

Jacob ran! He didn't look back! But on the way he slept under the stars with a rock for a pillow. While he slept, Jacob dreamed. He dreamed of a ladder leading up to heaven, with angels climbing up and down. Jacob heard God's voice and knew that he had God's blessing, as well as his father's.

50

Jacob loves Rachel

Genesis 29:1-20

Before he reached his uncle's house, Jacob met a beautiful shepherd girl called Rachel. He knew immediately that he wanted to marry her. When he found out that Rachel was Laban's daughter, Jacob promised to work for his uncle for seven years if Rachel could be his wife.

51
Laban tricks Jacob

Genesis 29:21-27

Jacob was happy to work hard if he could marry Rachel. But seven years later, when Jacob went to kiss his new wife, he found that Laban had tricked him! The woman under the veil was Rachel's older sister, Leah!

"It's our custom that the older sister gets married first," smiled naughty Uncle Laban.

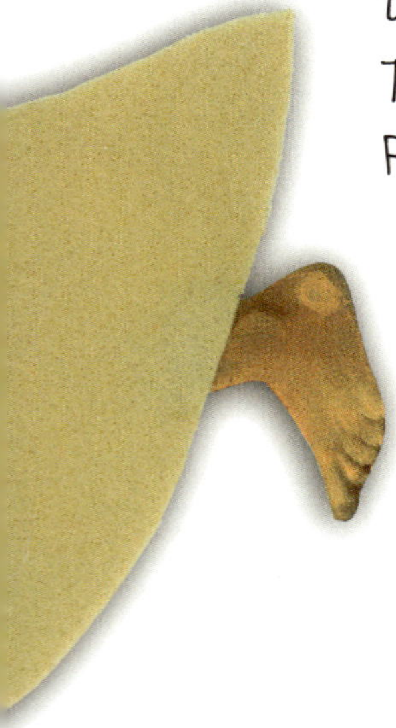

52

Jacob marries Rachel

Genesis 29:27-28

Jacob was very sad that Rachel was not his wife. But Laban told him that he could marry Rachel too – as long as he worked for another seven years! So, since many people had more than one wife at that time, Jacob also married Rachel. Now he had two wives.

53

Jacob's big family

Genesis 29:31-24

God blessed Leah with many children, and later, Rachel had two sons too. So Jacob had a large family of twelve sons and a daughter: Reuben, Simeon, Levi, Judah, Dan, Naphtali, Gad, Asher, Issachar, Zebulun, Dinah, Joseph and Benjamin.

54
Laban tries another trick

Genesis 30:25-36

The time came when Jacob wanted to take his family home. But Laban didn't want him to go. He knew that God had blessed him while Jacob was there. "Leave me when you have built up a herd of speckled or spotted animals," he said. Then Laban hid them all!

55

Spots and speckles

Genesis 30:37-43

Jacob was even trickier than Laban! He bred the sheep and goats so that soon, everywhere he looked, the sheep were black and white and every variation of spotted and speckled! When his herd was big and strong, Jacob crept away with his wives, his children and all his animals.

56

Jacob meets God

Genesis 32:24-32

One night, Jacob found himself wrestling, struggling in the darkness, with a stranger. When the sun rose, Jacob realized that he had met God – and that God had blessed him. Now Jacob was to be called Israel. His children were the children of Israel, and came to be known as the Israelites.

Friends and brothers

Genesis 33:1-17

That day, Jacob saw Esau coming toward him with 400 men! Jacob was frightened. What would Esau do? He told his family to wait while he met the army alone. But what was happening? Esau was running to Jacob and throwing his arms around him! Esau had forgiven his brother. Now they were friends.

58

Jacob's favorite son

Genesis 37:3-4

Joseph was Rachel's first-born son and soon he was Jacob's favorite. Jacob gave Joseph a beautiful colored coat as a gift and Joseph felt very special. But Joseph's brothers were not happy. They were jealous and angry – because they saw that their father loved Joseph more than them.

59
Joseph's strange dream

Genesis 37:5-8

One night, Joseph dreamed. He dreamed that he and his brothers were tying bundles of grain. Joseph's eleven brothers' bundles bowed down before his tall bundle. Did it mean something? Would Joseph one day rule over his brothers like a king? The brothers were cross and grumpy!

60

Sun, moon and stars

Genesis 37:9-11

Joseph dreamed again. This time the sun, the moon and eleven stars bowed down to him. Now Joseph's family were sure: one day the whole family would bow down before him. The brothers were very angry. They began to think of ways to forget Joseph for ever.

61

Angry brothers

Genesis 37:12-19

One day, Joseph's brothers were watching over their father's sheep in a faraway field. They had been gone for a long time, so Jacob sent Joseph to check if his brothers were safe. Joseph was happy to see his brothers, but his brothers were not at all happy to see him!

62

The plot against Joseph

Genesis 37:20-24

Joseph's brothers were not just jealous. They hated Joseph so much they wanted to kill him! But Reuben, the oldest brother, knew that was wrong. So he suggested they should throw him into a dry well for a while. The brothers ripped off his colored coat – and threw him in!

63
Sold to be a slave

Genesis 37:25-28

After a while, some spice traders came by on camels. Soon the brothers had twenty silver coins chinking in their hands – and Joseph was on his way to Egypt to be sold as a slave. They told Jacob that Joseph had been killed by a wild animal – and Jacob cried for months...

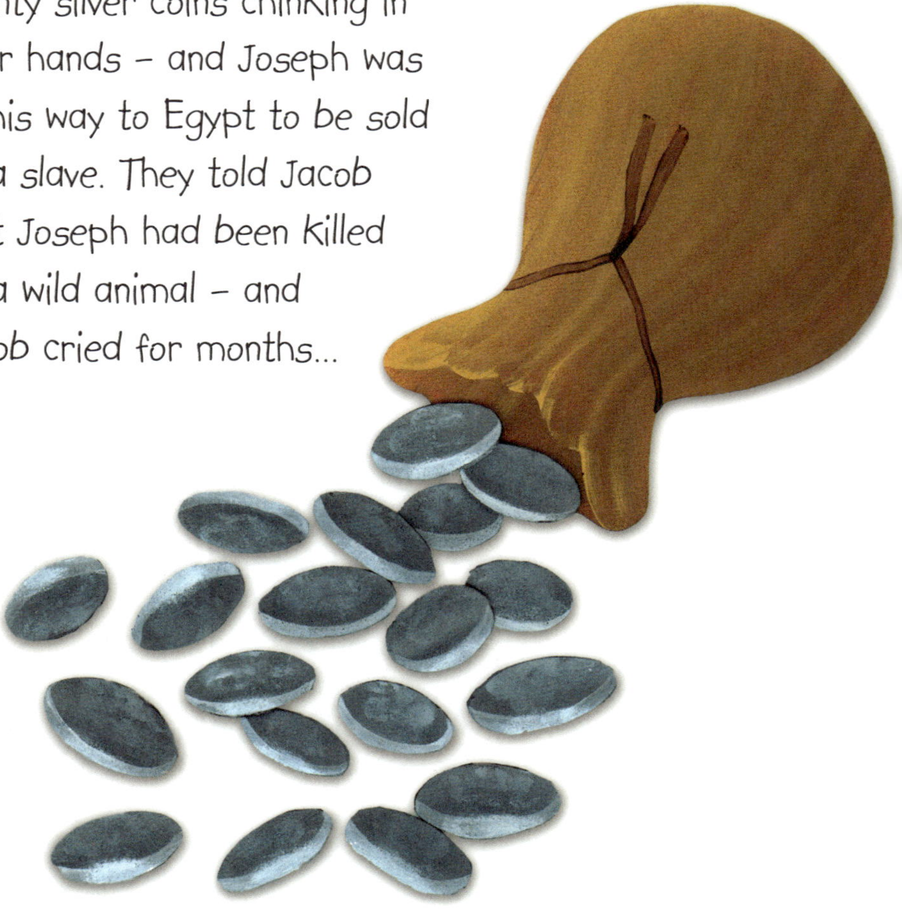

64

Far away from home

Genesis 39:1-7

The brothers may have forgotten Joseph, but God had not. Joseph was sold to Potiphar, who was a kind master to a good slave. Joseph worked hard and proved to be good at everything he did. Potiphar put Joseph in charge, and God blessed his house.

65

More bad news for Joseph

Genesis 39:7-20

Joseph was a handsome young man. Every day, Potiphar's wife would try to kiss him – and every day, Joseph would try to get away from her! Then one day Potiphar's wife told her husband lies about Joseph. Potiphar was angry and Joseph was thrown into prison.

66

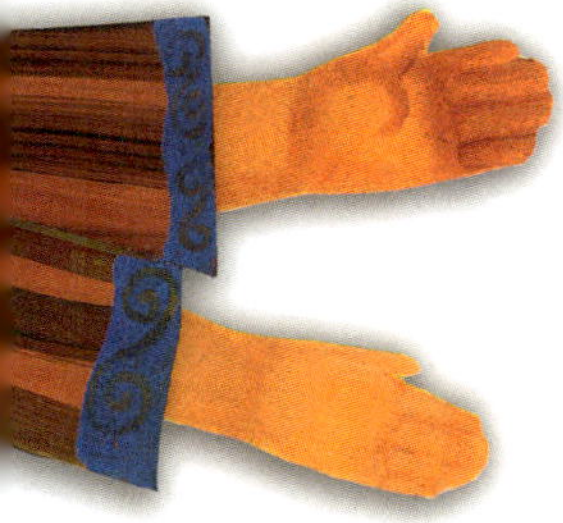

The baker's dream

Genesis 40:16-18

Even in prison, God blessed Joseph. One day, the king's baker and butler were thrown into prison too. Joseph listened as the baker told him about his dream: the baker had made three loaves of bread for the king, but the birds came along and ate them all. What could it mean?

67
The butler's dream

Genesis 40:1-23

The butler dreamed that the king drank wine he had made from three branches of grapes. What could that mean? Joseph told the butler good news: in three days, he would work again for the king. But he told the baker bad news: in three days, he would be hanged! And Joseph was right...

68
The king's dream

Genesis 41: 1-8

Two years later, it was the King's turn to have a strange dream. Seven fat, healthy cows were grazing by the Nile, when seven skinny, bony cows came up and ate them! Then he dreamed that seven scorched ears of grain swallowed up seven plump ears of golden grain. What could that mean?

Joseph amazes the king

Genesis 41:14-37

The butler remembered that Joseph understood the meaning of dreams. Joseph was brought out from the prison... and told the King that God was sending him a warning. First there would be seven years with wonderful harvests, but then there would be seven years of famine.

70

Joseph's new job

Genesis 41:38-49

Joseph told the king that he needed someone who would store the grain from the good harvests so his people would not be hungry when the famine came. The king placed a ring on Joseph's hand. He gave Joseph fine clothes to wear and put a gold necklace around his neck. Joseph would be that person!

71

A very powerful man

Genesis 41:53-57

The good harvests came to Egypt, followed by the famine, just as Joseph had said. The people of Egypt cried out to the king for food, and he said, "Go to Joseph." Once a slave, Joseph had become a powerful man in Egypt. He opened the storehouses of grain and made sure everyone had enough to eat.

72
Famine in Israel

Genesis 42:1-3

Back in Israel, people were also short of food. Jacob said to Joseph's ten older brothers, "You are hungry. I am hungry. Why don't you go to Egypt where there is grain for sale?" So Joseph's brothers went to Egypt, following the trail that Joseph had made many years before.

73

Dreams come true

Genesis 42:5-10

Joseph's brothers bowed low before the man with the ring on his hand and the gold necklace around his neck. They did not recognize him as the boy with the colored coat! "We are your humble servants," they said. "We are here to buy food." It was just like Joseph's dreams!

74

Joseph's trick

Genesis 42:11-38

Were Joseph's brothers the same cruel men who had wanted to kill him; who had sold him to be a slave? Joseph sent them home with lots of grain, but he hid the money they paid in their sacks. He took one brother hostage so they would come back with their youngest brother, Benjamin. And then... Joseph waited.

75

Benjamin goes to Egypt

Genesis 43:1-34

When the grain ran out, Joseph's brothers returned to Egypt with Jacob's youngest son. This time, Joseph put a silver cup into Benjamin's sack of grain so it looked as if he were a thief! Would the brothers defend Benjamin? Or would they leave him behind?

76
The silver cup

Genesis 44:1-34

The brothers were ready to go home when Joseph's servant shouted: "Stop! Some one has stolen my master's silver cup!" When the cup was found in Benjamin's sack, the brothers wept. "Please! Punish me, not Benjamin! It will break our father's heart!" they said.

77

Joseph forgives his brothers

Genesis 45:1-15

Joseph now knew for certain that his brothers were kinder men. He did not want to punish them, but to forgive them. He stopped pretending and hugged them all. "It was God's plan to bring me to Egypt," Joseph said. "It has saved our family from hunger in the famine."

78
Father and sons

Genesis 45:25-28; 47:5-12

Jacob nearly fell over when he heard the good news. "After all these years! My son Joseph is alive!" he said. The King let Joseph bring his father, all of his eleven brothers and their families to Egypt. They were at last one big, happy family.

79

Joseph's sons

Genesis 48:1-22

Jacob grew old and tired. He knew it was his time to die. Joseph took his own two sons, Manasseh and Ephraim, to see their grandfather. "May God bless these boys as he has blessed and looked after me," Jacob said. "One day God will take you all home to Canaan."

80

Joseph dies in Egypt

Genesis 50:22-26

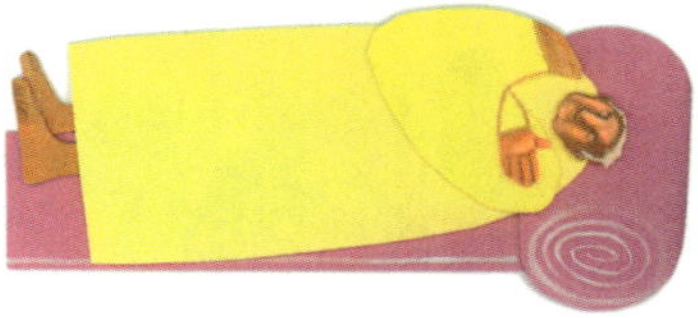

Joseph lived long enough to see his great, great grandchildren born. God had blessed him and all the children of Israel while they lived in Egypt. Before he died, Joseph told his brothers that God would look after them too, and take them back to the land God promised to Abraham one day.

81

The Israelites become slaves

Exodus 1:1-22

One day there was a new king who did not know what Joseph had done for Egypt. He only saw that the Israelites had grown to be too many people – and he was afraid. So the king made them all slaves. He made them work hard and he beat them. But still they grew stronger.

82

The baby in the basket

Exodus 2:1-3

Then the King ordered that every baby boy born to the Israelites should be thrown into the River Nile! One brave mother would not give up her baby son. She hid him from the soldiers as long as she could. Then she asked God to look after him, put him in a basket along the banks of the River Nile, and waited.

83

The Egyptian princess

Exodus 2:2-6

Miriam, the baby's sister, kept watch by the river. Soon she saw one of the King's daughters come to the river to have a bath. The princess heard the baby crying and asked her maid to fetch the basket. "Poor little baby," she said. "I want to keep him. I will call him Moses."

84

A mother for baby Moses

Exodus 2:7-9

Miriam was a clever little girl. "Shall I find an Israelite woman to care for the little baby?" she asked. The princess agreed, and Miriam ran home to get her mother. Moses then lived safely with his family until he was old enough to live in the palace with the princess.

85
Moses the Israelite

Exodus 2:10-14

Moses grew up in the palace and was educated like an Egyptian boy. But he never forgot who he was. One day, he was so angry when he saw an Israelite slave being beaten, that he killed the Egyptian slave driver. Then he was so afraid of being found out, that he ran away.

86

A home in the desert

Exodus 2:15-25

Moses went into the desert, where he met seven daughters fetching water from a well. When Moses helped the women, their father was grateful. He offered him one of his daughters to be his wife. Moses married and became a shepherd. He lived with his new family in the desert for over forty years.

87
The burning bush

Exodus 3:1-10

One day, while Moses was watching his sheep, he saw a bush that seemed to be on fire, but did not burn up. When he went closer to look, he heard the voice of God speaking to him from the flames. "Moses! My people need you. You must tell the king to set my people free."

88
Moses and Aaron

Exodus 4:10-20

Moses was first amazed, and then afraid. "But God," Moses said, "why would the king listen to me? And how can I talk to him? I wouldn't know what to say." God told Moses to find his brother, Aaron. God would help both Moses and Aaron to talk to the king.

89

God's message for the king

Exodus 7:1-13

"We have a message from the God of the Israelites, the God of all the world," Moses and Aaron told the king. "God says, 'Let my people go!'" But the king did not want to lose all his slaves. "Who is this God?" he replied. "I don't know him. Why should I do what he says?"

90

The river of blood

Exodus 7:14-25

The king would not obey God. So God sent plagues on the land of Egypt to make the king change his mind. God told Moses that Aaron should strike the water of river Nile with his stick. Suddenly, the deep green water turned bright blood red.

"Let my people go!" said God.

91

A plague of frogs

Exodus 8:1-15

The king said, "Yes!" but as soon as God took the blood away, the king changed his mind. "Ribbit! Ribbit!" Loud croaking noises were then heard all over the land of Egypt. There were frogs in the beds, frogs in the cooking bowls – frogs everywhere! "Let my people go!" said God.

92
Biting gnats

Exodus 8:16-19

The king said, "Yes!" but when God took the frogs away, the king changed his mind. So the dust of the earth gathered into a big cloud. The air filled with tiny biting gnats. Zzz! Phhttt! The people and their animals were covered from head to toe. "Let my people go!" said God.

93
Buzzing flies

Exodus 8:16-32

The king said, "Yes!" but when God took the gnats away, the king changed his mind. So God sent a swarm of flies. Buzz! Buzz! BUZZ! The flies covered the Egyptians but they didn't touch God's people, the Israelites. "Let my people go!" said God.

94

Dying animals

Exodus 9:1-7

The king said, "Yes!" but when God took the flies away, the king changed his mind. Now the cows, sheep, horses, donkeys, camels and all of the Egyptian livestock became ill and died. But the animals of the Israelites lived. "Let my people go!" said God.

95

Bumps and boils

Exodus 9:8-17

The king said, "Yes!" but then he changed his mind. How many chances did God have to give the king? Now the Egyptians began to break out in boils: red, itchy, pus-filled bumps popped up all over their skin so they were red-raw with scratching. "Let my people go!" said God.

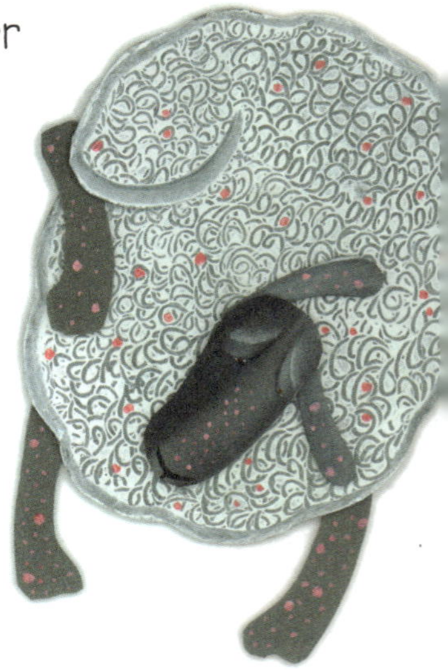

96
Hard hailstones

Exodus 9:18-35

The king said, "Yes!" but then he changed his mind. God sent a hailstorm. Sharp chunks of ice pelted the fields, destroying the plants and killing anyone who was outside. God sent thunder, hail and fire from heaven. "Let my people go!" said God.

97
A plague of locusts

Exodus 10:1-20

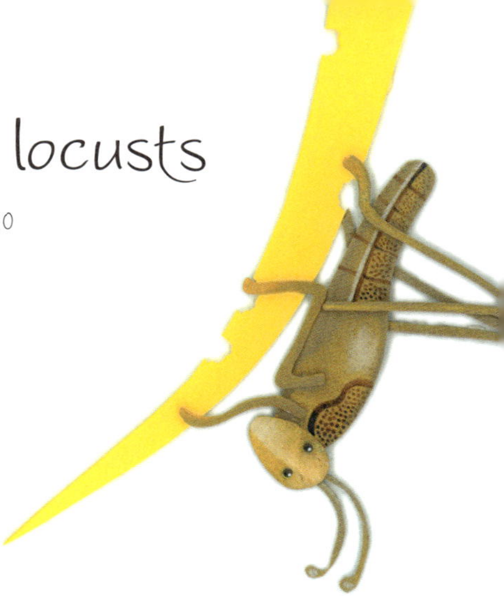

The king said, "Yes!" but then he changed his mind. Now even the king's servants were begging him to listen to God. An east wind blew, and the next morning, locusts covered all the land. They ate everything that the hail had not destroyed. "Let my people go!" said God.

98

Deep darkness

Exodus 10:21-29

The king said, "Yes!" but then he changed his mind. The once rich land was barren, but he would still not let the Israelites go. Then Moses stretched out his hand toward the sky and God brought darkness on the land for three whole days. "Let my people go!" said God.

99

The tenth plague

Exodus 11:1-10

The king said, "Yes!" but then he changed his mind. And this time he told Moses he never wanted to see him again. Now there would be no more chances for the king. God told Moses that at midnight all the first-born males in Egypt – both animals and children – would die.

100

The passover

Exodus 12:1-13

God said to Moses, "Tell my people to get ready for a long journey. They must eat a last meal of roast lamb, bitter herbs and bread made without yeast. They must mark their doorposts with the blood of the lamb. When I see this sign, I will pass over you. This final plague will not harm you." God kept his promise, and none of the Israelites were hurt.

101

The end of slavery in Egypt

Exodus 12:29-41

Cries of sadness were heard in every Egyptian house that night – even the king's. When he saw his own first-born son dead, he called for Moses and Aaron. "Take your people and go!" the king said. The Israelites gathered their families, all their possessions and followed Moses out of Egypt.

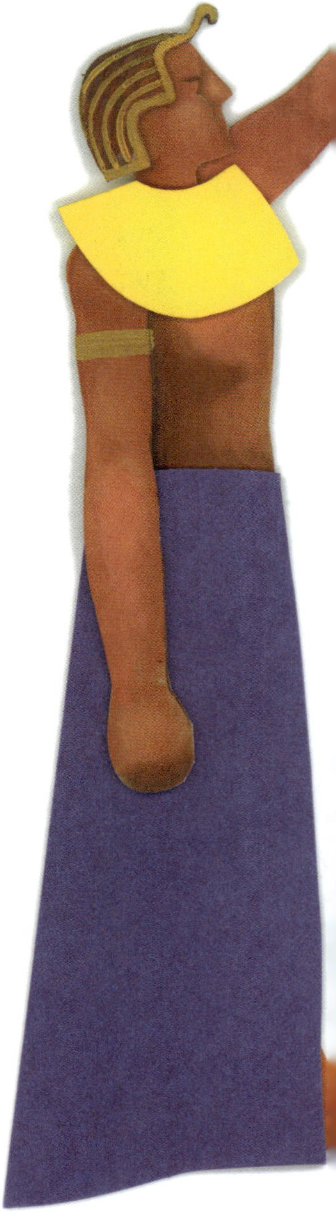

102

Pillar of cloud, pillar of fire

Exodus 13:17-22

Where were God's people going? Moses told them to trust God because he would lead them. God made a pillar of cloud for all the Israelites to follow during the day. They could see it from far away, even the families right at the back. At night, God led them with a pillar of bright fire that shone in the darkness.

103

Crossing the Red Sea

Exodus 14:1-22

Once the Israelites had gone, the king changed his mind! His army of horses and chariots quickly chased after them so the Israelites were trapped between the Egyptians and the Red Sea. What could they do? God told Moses to hold out his stick. The sea parted and the Israelites walked safely across to the other side.

104

Chariots underwater

Exodus 14: 23-31

The king's chariots caught up! They followed the Israelites on the dry sea bed. But when all of God's people were safely on the other side of the Red Sea, Moses raised his stick again. A flood of water washed over the Egyptians and their chariots. The Israelites thanked God for saving them.

105

Water in the desert

Exodus 15:22-27

Soon the Israelites were hot and thirsty and grumpy walking in the desert. Moses told them, "Trust God and he will bless us. He will give us everything we need." God led them to an oasis with twelve fresh springs of water and palm trees with sweet dates to eat.

106

The grumpy Israelites

Exodus 16:1-21

The Israelites kept finding reasons to complain. "We were better off as slaves in Egypt!" they moaned. "At least we had good food there!" Again God blessed them. He sent quails so they had meat in the evenings, and he sent sweet manna in the mornings.

107

Moses on the mountain

Exodus 19:1-25

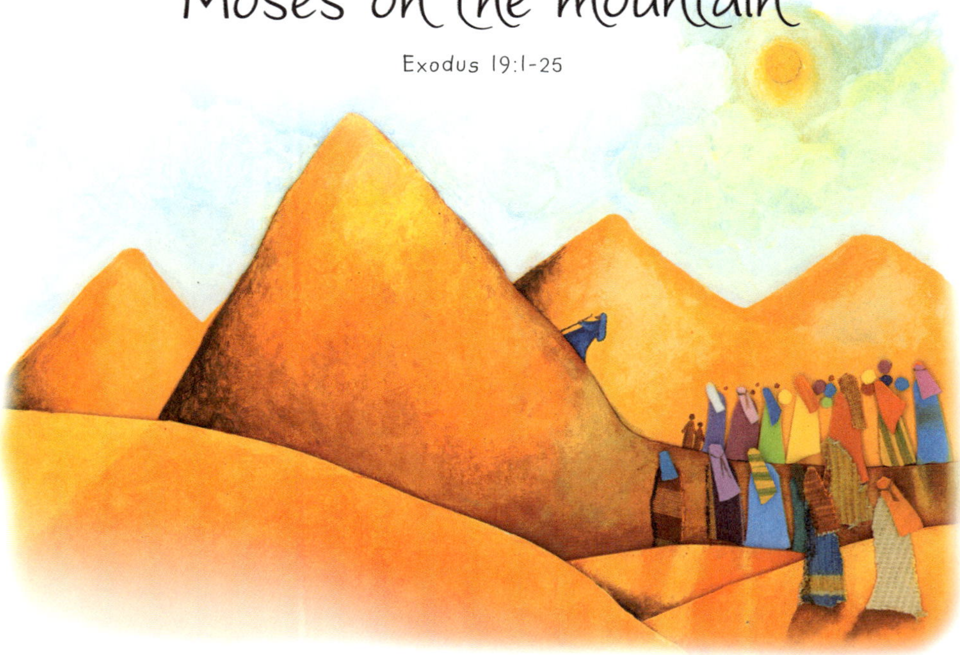

Day after day, month after month, the Israelites walked in the desert till they reached Mount Sinai which was covered in a thick cloud of smoke. Moses went up the mountain so he could meet with God. The people stayed at the bottom and waited. They heard thunder and lightning and a very loud trumpet sound.

108

Ten special rules

Exodus 21:2-12

God gave Moses rules to help them live.

1. God is the only God. Love him alone.
2. Don't make idols or worship things.
3. Respect God's name. It is special and holy.
4. Keep the Sabbath as a special day.
5. Love and respect your parents.

109
More rules on the mountain

Exodus 21:13-26

6.
Don't murder anyone.
7.
Don't steal someone else's wife or husband.
8.
Do not steal from anyone.
9.
Do not lie to anyone.
10.
Don't be jealous of other people's things.

The rules were written on two large stones. They were known as the Ten Commandments.

110

The golden calf

Exodus 32:1-6

Moses was on the mountain talking
with God about the Ten Commandments
for a long time. While he was away, t
he Israelites asked Aaron to make them
a god they could see, so they could worship it.
Aaron made them a golden calf from their
golden rings and jewellery.

111

Moses prays for the Israelites

Exodus 32:7-35

God saw the golden calf and was angry. "Forgive them," Moses prayed. "They are weak. They need to learn to trust you. Remember that you loved and cared for Abraham, Isaac and Jacob." Then Moses said to the people, "Whoever wants to love God and follow his ways, come with me!"

112

Priests to help the Israelites

Numbers 17 - 18

God gave the people priests to help them follow his special rules. They also helped them when they made mistakes and did bad things. God chose priests from the descendants of Jacob's son, Levi, and gave them rules to follow so the people knew how to worship him.

The ark of the covenant

Exodus 25:10-22

God wanted a special box to hold the stones on which the Ten Commandments were written. It was called the ark of the covenant, and was made of wood trimmed with gold. It had two gold rings on each side, so that it could be carried on poles wherever the Israelites went.

114

Spies in Canaan

Numbers 10 - 14

The Israelites walked through the desert for many years until they reached the land God had promised them. Then Moses sent twelve spies into the land of Canaan, one from each of the tribes descended from Jacob. The land was full of sweet water and good things to eat.

115

Living in the desert

Deuteronomy 31

Joshua and Caleb told everyone that God had given them a wonderful place to live. But the other ten spies were afraid of the fierce people who lived there! So the Israelites did not go to live in Canaan. They stayed in the desert for many more years. Moses, who was a very old man, died before God's people could live in Canaan.

116

God helps Joshua

Joshua 1:1-9

God chose Joshua to lead his people after Moses. Joshua had trusted God when the spies went into Canaan; Joshua knew he could trust God now. "Don't worry," said God. "I will help you as I helped Moses. Be strong. I will be with you wherever you go."

117

Rahab hides the spies

Joshua 2:1-7

Joshua sent two spies into the walled city of Jericho to find out about the people there. But the King found out they were there. Rahab hid the men under some flax on her roof. She sent the King's men another way and kept the spies safe till they could climb down the city wall and escape.

118

A promise for Rahab's family

Joshua 2:8-24

Why did Rahab help the spies? "Everyone knows about the amazing things your God has done," she told them. "We know God will give you this land. I ask only this: be kind to my family." The spies promised her family would be safe, and gave her a red ribbon to mark her window.

119

Crossing the River Jordan

Joshua 3:1-17

The Israelites had to cross the River Jordan, but there were no bridges or boats to get across. God told them what to do. The priests carrying the Ten Commandments walked into the river. As soon as their feet touched the ground, God stopped the river flowing.

120

On the other side

Joshua 4:1-24

The priests stood on the river bed until all the people had crossed over. God asked Joshua to choose a man from each tribe to carry a stone from the middle of the river. These twelve stones would always remind them of how God had helped them travel safely to Canaan.

121

The walls of Jericho

Joshua 5:13-15

Joshua sat by himself, thinking. The river was behind them. The strong walls of Jericho were in front of them. What were they to do next? Suddenly, an angel appeared! "Who are you?" Joshua asked. "I am the captain of God's army," he replied. Now Joshua knew that God would be there to help him.

122

Marching around the city

Joshua 6:1-11

Jericho was a fortress, with high walls to protect it. God told the Israelites to march around the city every day for six days. Marching in the middle of the army were seven priests blowing trumpets made out of rams' horns.

123

The walls fall down

Joshua 6:15-17

On the seventh day, God had told them to march around the city seven times. On the final time, Joshua signalled for everyone to shout with all their might! And the walls of Jericho crumbled! The people of Jericho ran, all except for Rahab and her family. They were kept safe.

124
The land of Canaan

Joshua 23:14-16

One by one, the cities fell until God's people could live there safely. Joshua had listened to God, and led his people well. But before he died, he warned them. "God has kept all his promises to us. Keep his commandments always and he will bless you and take care of you."

125

After Joshua

Judges 2:10

God's people settled in Canaan after Joshua died. The land was good and there was always food to eat. They built homes and cities, and there were new generations of Israelites. They were happy. But would they now remember that God had made it possible?

126

Rules forgotten

Judges 2:11-3:8

Soon the Israelites began to worship false gods. They were cruel to each other. God told his people that he would no longer protect them from their enemies unless they changed their ways. But they would not listen. They became slaves once more, as they had been in Egypt.

127

Deborah leads God's people

Judges 4:4-7

Long after Joshua, God spoke to his people through leaders called judges. Deborah was a prophetess and a judge. She sat under a palm tree, and told Barak that God wanted him to help his people by fighting the Canaanite general, Sisera. Barak was really scared!

128

A woman wins the battle

Judges 4:8-24

"I can't do it unless you come with me, Deborah," Barak said. "You should trust God! He will help you," Deborah answered. She warned Barak that now it would be a woman who would be praised for winning the battle. She was right. During the fighting, Sisera was killed by a woman named Jael, who hid him in her tent.

129

God chooses Gideon

Judges 6:11-35

The Israelites had broken God's rules again. And they were in trouble. Now the Midianites had stolen their livestock and food and forced the Israelites to hide in caves. God sent an angel to a man named Gideon. "God has chosen you to lead Israel against the enemy!"

130

Gideon needs a sign

Judges 6:36-38

"Are you sure?" Gideon asked. "I am not even a soldier!" Then Gideon asked for help. "I will put a woolly fleece on the floor. If there is dew on the fleece but not on the ground, I'll be sure you want me to do this." Next day the fleece was so wet, Gideon was able to squeeze a whole bowl of water out of it!

131

The dry fleece

Judges 6:39-40

Gideon still wasn't sure! Leading an army was a huge task... He said to God, "Please don't be angry with me, but this time, could you make the woolly fleece dry and the ground wet?" The next morning, the ground was wet with dew, but the fleece was perfectly dry. Now Gideon believed God would help him.

132

Too many men!

Judges 7:2-5

Gideon gathered an army of over 30,000 men! But God told him the army was too big. He told Gideon to send back anyone who was afraid. A lot of people went home! Then Gideon took the men who were left down to the water. Some knelt down to drink while some scooped up the water in their hands.

133

Gideon's small army

Judges 7:6-18

God wanted only the men who scooped up the water to fight in the army. Now there were only 300 men left! Gideon divided them into three groups. He gave each man a trumpet and a jar with a torch inside. In the middle of the night, they surrounded the Midianites.

134

God's victory

Judges 7:19-24

When Gideon gave the signal, they blew their horns, broke the jars so the light shone out, and shouted, "A sword for the Lord and for Gideon!" The Midianites were so confused, they ran in fear for their lives! Then the Israelites were free again to live safely in the land.

135

Naomi returns to Bethlehem

Ruth 1:1-18

Naomi moved with her husband and sons to Moab. When they died, she sent her sons' wives home to their parents. Naomi wanted to return to Bethlehem. But Ruth begged to stay with Naomi. "Your people will be my people. And I will worship your God," Ruth told her.

136

Ruth works in the fields

Ruth 2:1-3

Naomi was welcomed in her home town. But she still needed to find food to eat. God had made it part of the laws he gave to Moses that poor people could gather the leftover grain from the harvest so they would not be hungry. So Ruth worked hard in the fields all day so that she and Naomi would have enough to eat.

137

Boaz looks after Ruth

Ruth 2:4-12

Boaz owned the field where Ruth worked. He heard how kind she had been, looking after her dead husband's mother. "Gather as much as you need," he said kindly. When Naomi saw how much grain Ruth had collected, she knew that Boaz was a good man and that God had blessed them both.

138

Naomi becomes a grandmother

Ruth 4:9-17

Boaz saw that Ruth was good and kind and loyal. They became friends, and Naomi knew that soon there would be a wedding party. Naomi was very happy when Ruth and Boaz were married. She was even happier when they had a baby boy, and she held her little grandson in her arms.

139

Hannah prays for a baby

1 Samuel 1:1-20

Ruth and Naomi knew that having a baby was a sign that God had blessed them. So when, many years later, Hannah could not have a baby of her own, she was very sad. She prayed and prayed to God. Then she promised that if God gave her a son he would serve God in the temple.

140

God answers Hannah

1 Samuel 1:21-28

God heard Hannah's prayers. She was the happiest wife in Israel when she gave birth to baby Samuel! She loved him and looked after him well and when he was big enough, she took him to live in the temple just as she had promised. There Samuel learned how to serve God, with Eli, the priest.

141

The boy in the temple

1 Samuel 3:1-9

One night, Samuel heard a voice calling him. He woke Eli, saying, "Here I am!" But Eli said, "I didn't call you. Go back to sleep." It happened again! And then again! Then Eli understood. "God is speaking to you, Samuel," he said. "Listen to him, and do all he tells you."

142

Samuel the prophet

1 Samuel 3:19-21

God spoke and Samuel listened. Everyone knew they could trust Samuel, because he told them to do what God knew was best for them. With God's help, Samuel organized the Israelites into an army to defend them from the Philistines. So for a while, there was peace in the land and the people were happy.

143

A king for Israel

I Samuel 3:4-22

When Samuel grew to be an old man, the people of Israel said they wanted a king to rule them. "God is your king! God will look after you," Samuel told them. "Don't worry, Samuel. It is me they are rejecting," God said. "Give them what they ask for."

144

Saul's lost donkeys

1 Samuel 9:1-10

Saul's father had lots of donkeys. But they had wandered off somewhere. So Saul was sent to bring them home. He and his servant walked miles searching for them. Then the servant had a good idea. "Let's find Samuel, God's prophet. Maybe he will help us."

145

Samuel anoints Saul

1 Samuel 9:22-10:1

When Samuel saw a tall, handsome man coming toward him, God told him that Saul would be the people's king. "I know where your donkeys are – don't worry about them!" Samuel told Saul. "But I have more important news: I must anoint you God's chosen king of Israel."

146

Saul becomes king

I Samuel 10:17-27

Samuel gathered the twelve tribes to show them their new king. "Well, where is he?" they asked Samuel. Saul was so nervous, he was hiding among all the bags! But when he stood up, everyone was delighted with the king God had chosen. "Long live the king!" they shouted.

147

Saul knows best

I Samuel 15:1-35

At first everyone was happy. God helped Saul to be a good King, and the other nations stopped hurting God's people. King Saul was popular. Soon he began to think he could do things without God's help. He stopped listening to God. He did as he liked.

148

God chooses a new king

1 Samuel 16:1-9

Samuel knew that God wanted a good king, not just a powerful man. So he wasn't surprised when God sent him to Bethlehem to meet a man named Jesse who had eight sons. Jesse introduced the eldest of his sons. He was tall and strong. "This must be the one God has chosen," Samuel thought.

149

Samuel meets seven sons

I Samuel 16:9-12

God said to Samuel, "What a person looks like on the outside is not everything. What matters is whether they are good and kind and wise. I see what people are like when no one is looking at them." Samuel met seven of Jesse's sons, but none of them was God's chosen king.

150

God chooses David

I Samuel 16:13

"Do you have another son?" Samuel asked. "Yes," said Jesse. "My youngest son, David, is taking care of the sheep. I will send someone for him." When Samuel met David, God said, "This is the next king of Israel." So Samuel anointed David with oil, as a sign that one day he would be king.

151

Moody King Saul

I Samuel 16:14-18

King Saul couldn't sleep. He was grumpy and cross. He shouted at everyone. No one could do anything right. Then one of his servants said, "Perhaps some music would help you. I know a strong young man who loves God and plays the harp. His name is David."

152

David's song

Psalm 23

So David came to play the harp. His music soothed the king so much that Saul asked him to be in charge of his armor. David also wrote songs. "God is my shepherd," he sang. "He gives me everything I need. Nothing can frighten me, because God will take care of me."

153

Goliath, the champion

I Samuel 17:1-11

The Philistine army was always bothering the Israelites. One day, David heard the challenge that, day by day, the Philistine champion Goliath shouted at them. "Come out and fight me! I dare you!" Goliath was huge – over nine feet tall! Even the king was too scared to fight him.

154

David fights the giant

1 Samuel 17:31-58

But David wasn't scared. "You may have fancy armor, but I have the God of all the world to help me!" he shouted back. Then David took a smooth stone and slung it from his slingshot. It hit Goliath in the forehead and the giant fell down with a thud. The Israelites cheered! The Philistines ran away!

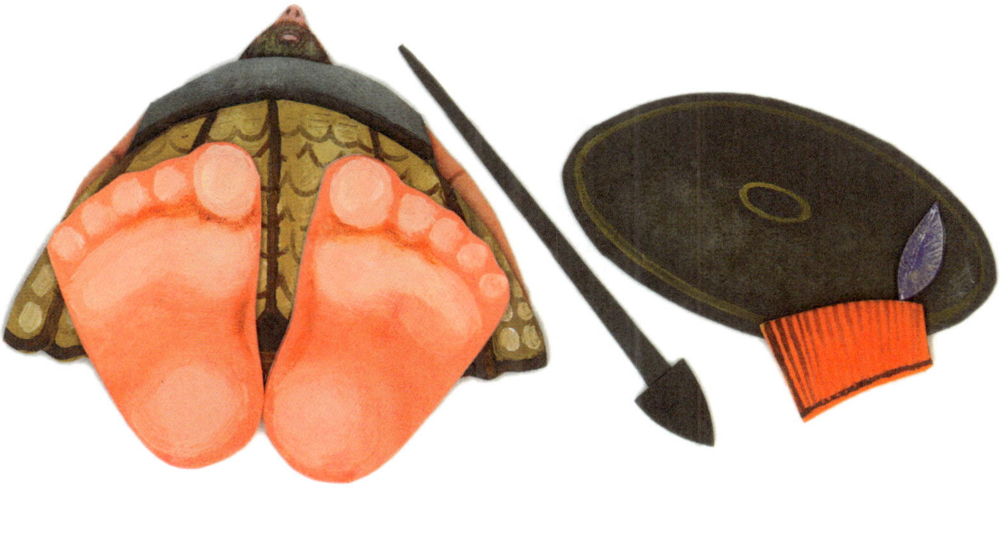

155

David is anointed king

1 Samuel 18:6-9, 2 Samuel 5:1-5

Soon, stories and songs about David's bravery became known among all the Israelites. King Saul became very jealous of David. He even tried to kill him! But God kept David safe. When King Saul died, the people asked David to be their king.

156

The king in Jerusalem

2 Samuel 6:1-19

The people loved King David. There was a king of Israel now who loved God and did good things. For a while, there was peace again in the land. David took the ark of the covenant with the Ten Commandments in it to the city of Jerusalem.

157

David's mistake

2 Samuel 11:1-27

One night, while David's army was away at war, David saw a beautiful woman. He found out that she was Bathsheba, the wife of Uriah. David wanted very much to meet Bathsheba. Then he made sure that Uriah was killed in battle so that Bathsheba was free to become his wife.

158

Nathan tells a story

2 Samuel 12:1-6

David knew that he had done something very wrong. He hoped no one else would find out. But God knew what Daniel had done. God sent Nathan to David. Nathan told David a story about a rich man who stole a poor man's only lamb. David was angry. "That rich man deserves to die!" David said.

159

David is sorry

2 Samuel 12: 6-13

Nathan looked at David. "But David," he said, "you are like that rich man. You are a king, yet you stole Bathsheba from Uriah, the soldier." Then David put his head in his hands and he cried. David was very, very sorry. "God is very sad because of what you have done," said Nathan. "But he will forgive you."

160

Bathsheba's baby sons

2 Samuel 12:14-25

Bathsheba had a baby son, but he became ill and died. David was very sad again. He was sure it was his fault for stealing Bathsheba from Uriah. Then God blessed David and Bathsheba with another son and they were happy once more. They named him Solomon.

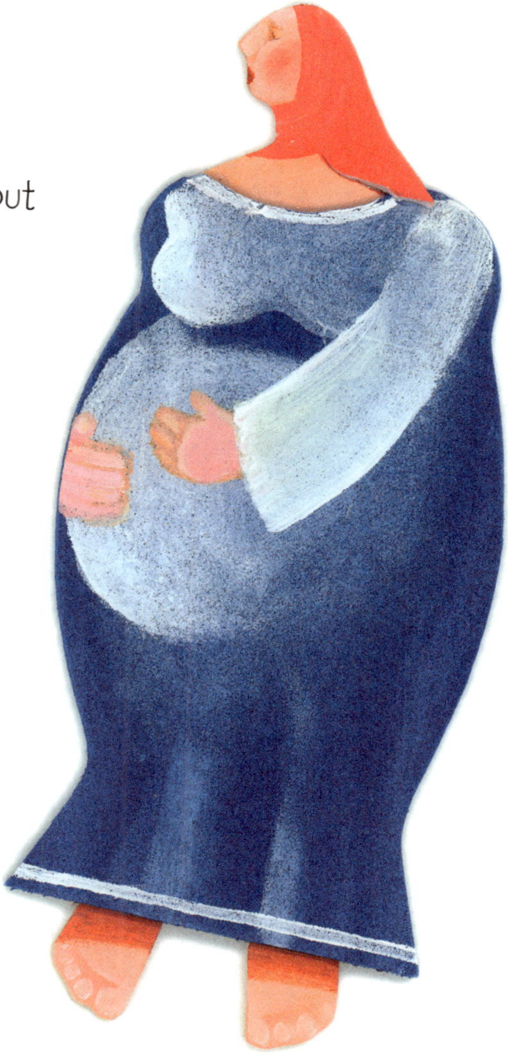

161

The next king of Israel

2 Samuel 22:1, 1 Kings 1:31-37

David was king for a long time. He wrote many poems and songs. Some were happy and told God how great he was. Some asked for God's help. When the time came for David to die, he asked to see Bathsheba and Nathan. "Make sure Solomon is the next king," he said. "He will listen to God."

162

Good advice for Solomon

1 Kings 1:38-40, 2:1-12

Before he died, David gave his son some advice. "Keep God's commandments and you will succeed in everything." David had learned the hard way, but he hoped Solomon would do better. Then Solomon was anointed with oil and declared King, just as his father before him.

163

God's gift to Solomon

1 Kings 3:5-15

One night in a dream, God said to Solomon, "Ask for anything you like and I will give it to you." Did Solomon ask to be rich? No. Did he ask to be famous? No. "Please give me a wise heart, so I can help your people," Solomon prayed. God made him the wisest man ever – and rich and famous too!

164

The two babies

1 Kings 3:16-25

Two women had given birth to baby boys. One baby had died. They came to see King Solomon. "The living baby is mine!" said one. "No, he's mine!" said the other. How would Solomon know who the real mother was? "Cut the baby in half," Solomon said. "Share it."

165

Solomon's wisdom

1 Kings 3:26-28

One of the women cried out, "Yes, cut the baby in half!" The other said, "No! Give her the baby! Don't hurt him!" Solomon gave the second woman the baby: the real mother would never let her child be hurt! Everyone heard about the king's wisdom. They knew that God had blessed him.

166

A house for God

1 Kings 5:13 – 6:38

Solomon built a temple in Jerusalem so the people could worship God there. It took thousands of men seven years to build it. It was made with stone walls panelled with wood and covered in gold. It was decorated with carved flowers and golden angels. It was beautiful.

167
Solomon's prayer

I Kings 8:22-66

When the ark of the covenant was brought to the temple, Solomon prayed. "I know you are too great to live in this house, dear Lord! But let your people come to worship you here, ask for your help in their need, and for your forgiveness when they do things that are wrong."

168

The queen of Sheba

I Kings 10:1-13

A queen from the faraway land of Sheba heard how wise Solomon was and came to Israel to find out for herself. When she saw his palace and heard the wise things he said, she gave him gifts of gold, precious stones and spices. "God has truly blessed you," she told him.

169

Ahab and Jezebel

1 Kings 16:29-33

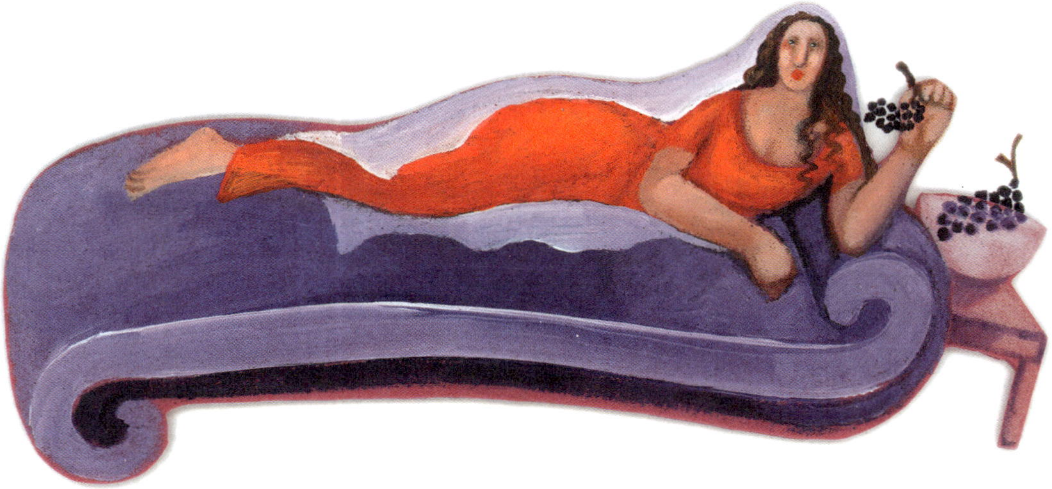

After Solomon died, there were kings of Israel who did not love God. King Ahab married a woman named Jezebel who worshipped a false god called Baal. Ahab built a temple to Baal and worshipped the false god too. Ahab broke many of God's ten commandments.

170

Elijah and the drought

1 Kings 17:1

God was not happy with Ahab. So he sent his prophet, Elijah, with a message for him. "God is the only true and living God. But you worship gods of wood and stone who can do nothing. Now God has decided that unless you change your ways and keep his commandments, he will send no more rain."

171

Ravens bring food

I Kings 17:2-6

King Ahab was very angry. Elijah was so afraid the king would kill him that he ran away! God told him where to find a place where he could get water from a brook to drink. Then God sent ravens to Elijah with bread each morning and with bread and meat each evening. God took care of Elijah.

The widow who shared

I Kings 17:7-12

When the brook dried up in the drought, God told Elijah to go to a village where a widow would help him. Elijah met the widow gathering sticks to make a fire and asked for food. "I am about to make bread for the last meal we will eat before we die," she said.

173

God provides

1 Kings 17:13-16

"Share your food with me and trust God," Elijah told the widow. She used the last of her flour and her last drop of oil to make bread for Elijah. But when she looked again, there was enough flour and oil for more bread! God made sure they did not go hungry until he sent rain again.

174

Elijah returns to King Ahab

I Kings 18:16-18

Three years passed without rain. Then Elijah went to meet King Ahab. "Here you are! The man who brought trouble to Israel!" said the King. Elijah answered, "You are that man! Are you ready yet to tell God you are sorry? Will you stop worshipping Baal and love God instead?"

175

Contest on Mount Carmel

1 Kings 18:20-21

Elijah told Ahab to gather all the prophets of Baal and meet on top of Mount Carmel. Elijah spoke to the Israelites gathered there: "Choose today whom you will worship. If the Lord is God, then follow him. But if Baal is god, then follow him."

176

No answer on the mountain

1 Kings 18:22-29

Elijah challenged the prophets of Baal to prepare a sacrifice to their god. Elijah would do the same. "Call on your god to light your altar with fire," Elijah said. The prophets of Baal danced and shouted to their god, and shouted and danced, but nothing happened; nothing at all.

177

Elijah's altar

1 Kings 18:30-35

Then Elijah built an altar of twelve stones with a small trench around it. "Fill four jars of water and pour them over the wood of this altar. Do it again and again until everything is soaking wet." How could fire burn on the altar with all that water over it?

178

God sends fire and rain

1 Kings 18:36-46

Elijah prayed. "Oh Lord, show these people that you alone are God." Suddenly the altar lit up with fire! God had answered Elijah. God was real! God answered prayers. The people knelt down and worshipped the true and living God. Then God sent first a little cloud, then big rain clouds. The drought was over.

179

Elijah has a helper

1 Kings 19:14-21

God told Elijah he needed someone to help him. God sent him to find Elisha, who was plowing in the fields near his home. Elisha left home and went to help Elijah serve God. Soon people knew that Elisha would be the next prophet. God would speak through him.

180

Chariot of fire

2 Kings 2:1-11

Elisha knew that Elijah was nearly at the end of his life. They were at the River Jordan, and Elijah divided the water for them to cross on dry land. Suddenly, a chariot of fire drawn by horses carried Elijah away to heaven in a whirlwind! Elijah had gone to be with God.

181

The little servant girl

2 Kings 5:1-3

An Israelite girl had been taken captive to work as a servant in the house of Naaman, a captain of the Aramean army. Naaman had a skin disease called leprosy. "I wish my master would visit the prophet Elisha," she whispered to her mistress. "God could cure my master."

182

Naaman visits Elisha

2 Kings 5:1-10

Naaman took a letter to the King of Israel asking him to cure his leprosy. "How can I do that?" shouted the king. "Am I God?!" But Elisha heard of it, and told the king to send Naaman to him. But did Elisha meet Naaman and treat him as an important visitor?

183

Naaman is healed

2 Kings 10-14

Elisha just sent a message! "Wash seven times in the River Jordan and you will be healed." Naaman was horrified. There were better rivers where he came from! But Naaman's servant encouraged him to do this simple thing. So Naaman did – and his skin was like brand new. God had healed him.

184

Jonah is sent to Nineveh

Jonah 1:1-2

Long after Elisha, there was another prophet called Jonah. "Go to Nineveh and warn the people there that I have seen the terrible things they do. They must change their ways!" said God. The people of Nineveh were cruel and keen on fighting. Jonah did not want to go!

185

Jonah runs away

Jonah 1:3

What did Jonah decide to do? He ran away! He boarded the first boat leaving Joppa going in the opposite direction of Nineveh. He found somewhere below deck to hide away – and he fell asleep! Jonah forgot that you can't hide from God.

186

Storm at sea

Jonah 1:4-6

Suddenly a massive storm rocked the boat. "Whoo-ooo!" went the howling wind. "Crra-ack!" went the loud thunder. The sailors were so afraid, they threw the cargo overboard to lighten the ship. "Wake up, Jonah and pray for help!" the sailors shouted to Jonah.

187

Man overboard!

Jonah 1:9-12

As the sailors clung on for their lives, Jonah realized the storm was all his fault. "I am running away from my God," he said. "The storm will only stop raging if you throw me overboard!" The sailors did not want to hurt Jonah – but they didn't want to die. They threw him into the sea.

188

Swallowed by a fish

Jonah 1:15-17

Jonah fell down, down, down into the sea, and straight away the storm stopped raging. But God didn't let Jonah die. He sent a great big fish to swallow him up, and Jonah sat in the smelly belly of the fish for three days and three nights. And Jonah prayed to God.

189

Jonah's prayer

Jonah 2:1-10

"Every time I needed you, you were there for me," Jonah prayed. "When I fell into the deep water, you rescued me. I promised to serve you, dear God, and I will. Only you have the power to save!" Then the fish spat Jonah out on to dry land. And God sent Jonah back to Nineveh.

190

God's message for Nineveh

Jonah 3:1-4

As Jonah approached the huge city of Nineveh, he shouted out, "God says that in forty days, Nineveh will be destroyed!" Did the people attack Jonah? Did they ignore him? No! They stopped and listened and heard God's message. They were sorry for the wrong things they had done.

191

God forgives

Jonah 3:5-10

The people of Nineveh begged God for forgiveness. Even the king of Nineveh tore off his beautiful robes and wore itchy sackcloth to show God that he was sorry. God saw that the people had changed their ways. He saw that they were sorry and he forgave them.

192

Jonah's anger

Jonah 4:1-11

Was Jonah happy that God had forgiven the people? No. Jonah sulked. He thought they deserved to die. A vine had grown up to give Jonah shade, but then it had withered and died. God said: "Jonah, you didn't make or take care of that vine, but you cared when it died. I did make these people. I care what happens to them."

193

God chooses Jeremiah

Jeremiah 1:1-10

God chose Jeremiah to be his prophet many years after Jonah. The people had again forgotten his commandments. They worshipped false gods again. Jeremiah was young. "I loved you even before you were born," said God. "I have plans for you and I will help you. I will tell you what to say."

194

The clay on the potter's wheel

Jeremiah 18:1-6

God sent Jeremiah to a potter's house. The potter's wheel spun around, but the clay went a little wrong. What a mess! But the potter simply reshaped it so it made a beautiful pot. Jeremiah saw that God was like the potter. Even if things had gone wrong, God could change his people into something better.

195

Words in the fire

Jeremiah 36:1-28

Jeremiah warned the people to keep God's commandments, but no one listened. So Jeremiah wrote down everything God told him on a long scroll and sent it to the king. The king burned it without even reading it! Jeremiah sat down... and began writing all over again.

196
God's warning

Jeremiah 37:1-10

What was God's message? God warned Jeremiah that the king of Babylon would destroy Jerusalem and make prisoners of God's people. Jeremiah pleaded with them to listen to God's warning and leave the city. But everyone ignored him – till it was too late.

197

The deep, dark vault

Jeremiah 37:11-21

The Babylonians started to attack. Surely the king would listen now? But instead, Jeremiah was put into a dark prison. The king came secretly to find out if God had told Jeremiah some good news. But Jeremiah said, "God warned you before. He tried to tell you but you refused to listen. The Babylonians will win!"

198

A lonely, muddy well

Jeremiah 38:1-6

The king's officials heard what Jeremiah had said. "This man is a troublemaker! He's upsetting everyone!" They were so angry that they threw Jeremiah into an empty well to die. Jeremiah sank deep into the mud at the bottom. Poor Jeremiah! Being God's prophet was not an easy job...

199

Rescue at last

Jeremiah 38:7-16

A man heard what had happened to Jeremiah and went to the king, "Please, sir, don't let Jeremiah die." So the king sent thirty men to pull him out of the well. Again the king asked for good news. "I can only tell you what God tells me – and you don't listen!" said Jeremiah.

200

Jerusalem is captured

Jeremiah 38:17-39:2

Jeremiah told King Zedekiah to surrender to the Babylonians, and he and his family would live. The King was afraid but he wouldn't trust God. So when the Babylonians captured Jerusalem, the king was blinded and taken away in chains. All his sons were killed.

201

God looks after Jeremiah

Jeremiah 39:3-12

Now Solomon's beautiful temple was in ruins and the precious things inside stolen. The palace had been burned down and the walls of Jerusalem destroyed. Many of the people had been taken to Babylon to work for the king there. But Jeremiah was set free. He decided to stay and take care of the people who were left behind.

202

Captives in Babylon

Daniel 1:1-13

Daniel and his three friends were captives from Jerusalem. When they were given rich food to eat so they could work in the Babylonian court, Daniel asked for vegetables and water. He did not want to break God's commandments and knew that the meat had been offered to idols.

203

Nebuchadnezzar's dream

Daniel 2:1-12

King Nebuchadnezzar had dreams that kept him awake at night. His magicians said, "Tell us your dreams. We'll tell you what they mean." But the king said, "If you're so clever, tell me what I dreamed first – or die!" The magicians trembled. They knew they couldn't do this.

204

God helps Daniel

Daniel 2:25-30

Daniel spoke to King Nebuchadnezzar. "No wise man or magician can tell you your dream. But there is a God in heaven who can. I have prayed to him for help and he has answered me. Now I can show you his power by telling you what you dreamed."

205
A very tall statue

Daniel 2:31-45

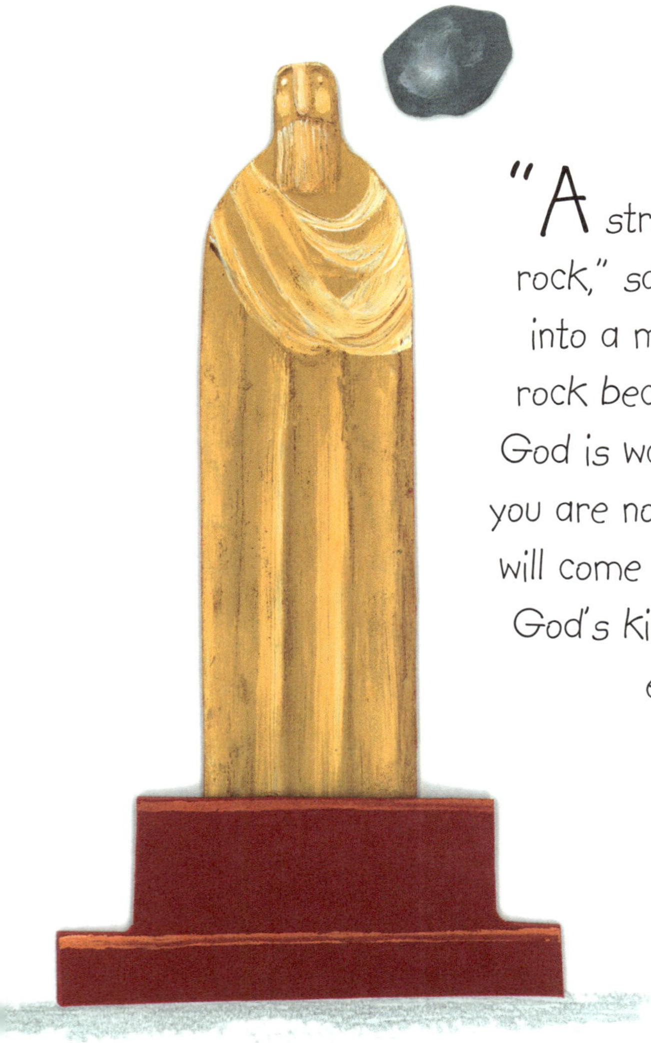

"A strong statue was hit by a rock," said Daniel. "It smashed into a million pieces. Then the rock became a great mountain. God is warning you that although you are now great, one day, others will come and destroy you. Finally, God's kingdom, which will never end, will come."

206

Shadrach, Meshach and Abednego

Daniel 3:1-22

King Nebuchadnezzar was pleased with Daniel – but he soon forgot God's warning and made a huge golden statue of himself. "Everyone must worship my statue!" he said. But Shadrach, Meshach and Abednego would worship only God. So they were thrown into a fiery furnace.

207

The fiery furnace

Daniel 3:24-29

God looked after Shadrach, Meshach and Abednego so the flames did not burn them. He sent an angel to protect them. King Nebuchadnezzar ordered the three men to come out of the fire. He praised God, who had the power to save them because they would die rather than worship a false god.

208

Daniel is forgotten

Daniel 5:1-2

Belshazzar became king after his father and Daniel was forgotten at court until... the new king threw a party for a thousand of the most important people in Babylon. He decided to use the beautiful gold and silver goblets that his father had taken from the temple in Jerusalem.

209

The writing on the wall

Daniel 5:3-7

While King Belshazzar and his guests drank wine from the beautiful goblets, and praised the gods they believed in, of gold and silver, wood and stone, the king saw the fingers of a man's hand write on the wall. King Belshazzar grew pale with fear! What was happening?

210
God speaks through Daniel

Daniel 5:13-29

None of the king's magicians knew what the message said. But they remembered Daniel. "God has counted the days you will be king," Daniel read. "They are over! God has tested you, and you have not passed the test. Your kingdom will be given to the Medes and the Persians."

211

Daniel's enemies

Daniel 6:1-4

Daniel was right. All he said came true. That very night, Belshazzar was killed and Darius the Mede became king. King Darius asked Daniel to help govern the kingdom. He was so pleased with everything Daniel did that he wanted him to have even more power... Daniel had a great friend – but also plenty of jealous enemies.

212

Plots against Daniel

Daniel 6:5-9

How could Daniel's enemies get him into trouble? They knew that Daniel loved God. They began to form a clever plan. They told King Darius how great he was. They persuaded the king to pass a law. If someone prayed to anyone but him, that person would be thrown into a den of lions!

213
Daniel prays

Daniel 6:10-15

What would Daniel do? Daniel did what he did every day. He went home and prayed to God. His enemies' plot had worked! They went straight to the king. Darius was sad. He did not want to hurt Daniel, but he knew that he had made the law and the law could not be changed.

214

Daniel in the lions' den

Daniel 6:16-21

Daniel was taken away and thrown to the lions. The door was locked tight! "Grrrr!" went the hungry beasts. King Darius shouted through the door, "May your God save you, Daniel!" The next morning, when Darius ran to the lions' den, Daniel called out, "May you live forever, King Darius! I am still here!"

215

God saves Daniel

Daniel 6:22-28

"God sent his angel to shut the lions' mouths," said Daniel. "The lions have not hurt me at all." King Darius made sure Daniel was released from the den. Then he issued a new law. "From now on, all people should respect Daniel's God, because he alone has the power to save, even from the mouths of lions."

216

Nehemiah's plan for Jerusalem

Nehemiah 2:1-8

It was many years since the Israelites had lived in Jerusalem together. Nehemiah, now the cupbearer in Babylon to the new King Artaxerxes, was very sad. He wanted to go home to Jerusalem, and rebuild its walls and gates. He prayed for God's help, and asked the king if he could go.

217
Help from the king

Nehemiah 2:11-20

It was a miracle! The king not only said Nehemiah could go, he sent him with special letters so he could buy supplies to do the work! Nehemiah went to Jerusalem and planned what could be done. He encouraged the people there, telling them all how God had answered his prayers.

218

The walls are rebuilt

Nehemiah 3:1-6:19

The people now had something very special. They had hope. They repaired the walls of Jerusalem and built new city gates. When they were afraid their enemies would attack them, Nehemiah reminded them that God was on their side. Together they fixed the walls in fifty-two days!

219

The Israelites weep

Nehemiah 8:1-12

As the people of Jerusalem came together inside the walls, Ezra brought out the book of the law of Moses. He reminded the people of God's commandments. They wept when they realized how they had broken his laws and disappointed God. Then they thanked him for bringing them home!

220

A Savior for God's people

Malachi 4:4-6

It had been a long journey from the first time people disobeyed God in the Garden of Eden until now. God sent Malachi to tell his people that he would send someone to show them how much he loved them and to give them a chance to put everything right. God would send someone to save them, a Savior.

The New

Testament

221

Elizabeth and Zechariah

Luke 1:5-7

God always keeps his promises. Hundreds and hundreds of years after Malachi, guess what? God made Zechariah, the priest, and his wife, Elizabeth, part of his plan. Elizabeth and Zechariah did not have any children – but they were in for a *surprise*.

222

The angel in the temple

Luke 1:8-22

Zechariah was working in the temple when an angel appeared! "This is God's message," said the angel Gabriel. "You're going to be father to a baby called John." Zechariah could not believe it! "As you have doubted God's promise, you will be unable to speak until your baby is born," said Gabriel.

223

A surprise for Mary

Luke 1:26-38

Six months later, Gabriel visited Elizabeth's young cousin, Mary. "You shall have a child named Jesus, and he will be called the Son of God," Gabriel said. Mary felt afraid. "But I'm not even married yet." Gabriel said, "Don't worry. Nothing is impossible for God."

224

A visitor for Elizabeth

Luke 1:39-45

Mary had to tell someone the news! She went to see Elizabeth as Gabriel had told her that Elizabeth was also having a baby. "Hello!" Mary called, and the baby inside Elizabeth kicked with joy! "I'm so lucky that the mother of the Savior is here visiting me!" said Elizabeth. "God has done something very wonderful."

225

Elizabeth's baby boy

Luke 1:57-66

Months later, Elizabeth gave birth to her little son. Just as Gabriel had told them, they named him John. Zechariah, who had been quiet for so long, found he could speak once more. How did John fit into God's plan? John would tell people that Jesus was coming! He would tell them to get ready.

226

God comforts Joseph

Matthew 1:18-25

Mary was pregnant. Joseph had planned to marry her but now he was worried. Could her story about an angel be true? Then one night Joseph dreamed that an angel spoke to him. "Don't worry, Joseph. Marry Mary. She needs you to help take care of God's son."

227

The Emperor counts his people

Luke 2:1-5

In those days, the Israelites were ruled by Romans. Caesar Augustus ordered everyone to return to the place where their families came from to be counted. So Joseph took Mary with him to Bethlehem, the city where King David had lived long, long ago.

228

The inn in Bethlehem

Luke 2:6-7

Bethlehem was full of people! The streets were crowded, and Joseph and Mary were tired from traveling. Mary knew that her baby would soon be born and she was anxious to stop and rest. There was no room for them at the inn, so Joseph found a stable where they could stay.

229
The baby in the manger

Luke 2:7

It was quiet in the stable – just the snuffly noises of the animals sleeping. Then there were the cries of a new-born baby, "Waa, waa..." Mary's little boy was born. Mary wrapped Jesus tightly in clean clothes to keep him warm and made a bed for him in the manger.

230

Shepherds on the hillside

Luke 2:8-11

There were shepherds watching their sheep nearby. Suddenly they were surprised by an angel who appeared on the hillside in front of them. "Don't be afraid," said the angel. "I bring good news! Jesus, your Savior, has been born in Bethlehem. You will find him lying in a manger."

231

The song of the angels

Luke 2:12-14

Suddenly, the sky was full of angels, lighting up the dark night sky. "Glory to God who lives in heaven, and peace to everyone who lives on earth," they sang. The sound of the angels was the most beautiful music the shepherds had ever heard.

232

The good news about Jesus

Luke 2:15-20

The shepherds could not wait to go to Bethlehem. They found baby Jesus lying in a manger and praised God for his birth. Then they told Mary and Joseph about the angels and their message. In fact, they told everyone they met about the good news that Jesus was born!

233

Simeon meets Jesus

Luke 2:21-34

Mary and Joseph took Jesus to the temple in Jerusalem to offer God two pigeons and thank him for his safe birth. An old man named Simeon took the baby from them and laughed with joy. "God told me that I would see the Savior before I died! And here he is!"

234

The star in the East

Matthew 2:1

A new star appeared in the sky when Jesus was born. Wise men, gazing at the stars and studying their positions, saw the star and believed that it meant a new king had been born. They decided to take him gifts. They followed the star to find the new-born king.

235

The wise men's journey

Matthew 2:2

The wise men traveled a long way from their home in the East until they arrived in Jerusalem. They were looking for a king, so they went to King Herod's palace. "Where is the baby born to be king of the Jews?" they asked. "We have come to worship him."

236

Grumpy King Herod

Matthew 2:3

King Herod was already king of Judea. But he was not a wise or a kind king. "A baby?" he thought. "There is room for only one king here!" So Herod asked his priests where the prophecies said that a king would be born. "From Bethlehem," came the answer.

237

The baby in Bethlehem

Matthew 2:4-8

King Herod smiled sweetly at the wise men and told them to look for the king in Bethlehem. "And when you find this special baby, this king of the Jews, please come back to tell me, so that I can worship him too."

238

Wise men find Jesus

Matthew 2:9-10

The wise men mounted their camels and continued their journey. "Look!" one of the wise men shouted. "There's the star again!" They followed the star until it seemed to twinkle above a house in Bethlehem. There they found Jesus with his mother, Mary.

239

Gifts for the baby king

Matthew 2:11

The wise men bowed down and worshipped Mary's little boy. Then they offered the gifts they had brought with them: gold, frankincense and myrrh. Such expensive gifts! Mary was surprised. When she was alone again, she wondered about what it could all mean.

240

Wise men dream

Matthew 2:12

The wise men left the little family and prepared for their journey home again. But God spoke to them in a dream and warned them not to go back the way they had come – through Jerusalem. King Herod was dangerous, and had been plotting how he could harm Jesus!

241

Runaways in Egypt

Matthew 2:13

God did not only warn the wise men about Herod. "Joseph!" God said that night. "Take Mary and Jesus and run away to Egypt! Herod is going to search for your child and try to destroy him." Joseph did not wait to think about it. They left that night.

242

A home in Nazareth

Matthew 2:19-23

Jesus grew up in Egypt. When Herod died, God spoke to Joseph in another dream and told him it was safe to take his family back to his own country. Mary and Joseph started the long journey, and finally settled in Nazareth in the area of Galilee.

243
Journey to Jerusalem

Luke 2:41-43

Every year, Joseph and Mary went with many other people from Nazareth to Jerusalem for the Passover festival. It was a wonderful time of year. There was singing and praying and parties to celebrate the time when Moses led the Israelites out of Egypt.

244
Jesus is lost

Luke 2:44-45

When Jesus was twelve years old, Mary and Joseph lost him in Jerusalem! They were on the journey home, each perhaps thinking that Jesus was with another member of the party of friends and family. When they couldn't find him, they went anxiously back to Jerusalem.

245

Jesus is found

Luke 2:46-52

It took three days of searching to find Jesus. They must have been frantic with worry! But when Mary and Joseph found him in the temple, his answer amazed them. "I was here, in my Father's house." Jesus had been talking to the teachers about God, his Father.

246

Elizabeth's son, John

Matthew 3:1-4

While Jesus was growing up, John had grown up too. John lived in the desert and was a prophet. He told people to turn away from the bad things they were doing and to keep God's commandments. He wore an itchy shirt of camel hair and lived on locusts and wild honey.

247

John's message

Luke 3:11-14

"If you love God, show it by the good things you do," said John. "Share your food with anyone who is hungry. If you have more clothes than you need, share them with someone who doesn't have enough. Be honest; don't tell lies about people."

248

John the baptist

Matthew 3:7-12

People asked John to baptize them in the River Jordan. "I baptize you with water to show that you are sorry and want God to forgive you. It's a bit like being washed clean," said John. "But look out for someone coming soon who will baptize you with the Holy Spirit."

249

John baptizes Jesus

Matthew 3:13-17

One day, Jesus came to be baptized by John. "But you have done nothing wrong! You don't need to say sorry. Instead, you should baptize me!" John said. But Jesus asked John to baptize him anyway. When he did, they all heard God's voice say, "This is my son. I love him."

250

A nasty test for Jesus

Matthew 4:1-4

Jesus really hadn't done anything wrong. But here was the devil to test him in the desert. Jesus had nothing to eat for forty days and his tummy was very rumbly. The devil said, "If you really are God's son, turn these stones into bread to eat." Jesus replied, "People need much more than food to live."

251

Another nasty test

Matthew 4:5-7

Then the devil took Jesus to the tippy top of the temple and said, "If you really are God's son, throw yourself down. Hasn't God promised that he will save you?" But Jesus said, "Yes, he will save me, but it's wrong to put God to the test. I will not do it."

252

The final nasty test

Matthew 4:8-11

Then the devil took Jesus to a very high mountain. It was so high, Jesus could see all the kingdoms of the world. "I will give you all of this," the devil said, "if you will only bow down and worship me." But Jesus said, "No! Get away from me! I will worship God, and God alone."

253

Friends of Jesus

Luke 5:4-6

Jesus watched the fishermen on Lake Galilee. "Throw your nets into the deep water," Jesus told Peter and Andrew. "You will catch lots of fish." Peter replied. "We fished all night and caught nothing! But we'll do it if you want us to." As soon as the two brothers put the nets into the water, they were filled with fish!

254

The fishing net that nearly burst

Luke 5:7-11

James and John were also in their boats on Lake Galilee. They went to help Peter and Andrew – and soon both boats were full of silvery wriggling fish! "Follow me," Jesus said. "You will catch men and women instead of fish." The four fishermen decided to follow Jesus from that day on.

255

Wedding in Cana

John 2:1-4

A wonderful wedding was happening in the village of Cana. Mary was invited, and Jesus and his friends went too. Everyone was having a great time celebrating, until Mary noticed that there was no more wine left. The bride and groom would be embarrassed! Perhaps Jesus would help them?

256

Miracle in Cana

John 2:5-10

Jesus asked the servants to fill six huge waterpots to the brim with water. Then he asked them to offer some to the person in charge of the feast. When the head waiter tasted it, it was no longer water, but the most delicious wine! It was a miracle!

257
Jesus preaches in Nazareth

Luke 4:14-30

Jesus went into the synagogue in Nazareth where he had grown up. "God has sent me to help the poor and heal the deaf and blind. God has sent me to show people how to live in a way that pleases him," Jesus said. But people shook their heads. This was only Mary's son. They could not believe it.

258

Four Friends

Mark 2:1-2

It was different in Capernaum. So many people wanted to hear what Jesus had to say that the house he was in was overflowing! Four men wanted Jesus to help their friend who couldn't walk. What could they do? There seemed to be no way for them to get inside.

259
The hole in the roof

Mark 2:3-4

There were stairs outside the house, leading to the flat roof. The men climbed up, carrying their friend on a mat. Then they made a large hole in the roof! Everyone looked up at the bits falling down on them. They were very surprised when a man was gently lowered to the floor.

260

The man is healed

Mark 2:5-12

Jesus smiled at the kind friends above him. He smiled at the man who couldn't walk. Then he told the man to get up, pick up his bed, and go home. And the man did! The religious leaders frowned and shook their heads. But everyone was amazed at what Jesus had done.

261

Jesus chooses Matthew

Matthew 9:9-13

Jesus saw Matthew at his work collecting taxes. "Follow me!" Jesus said, and Matthew followed him. But some people shook their heads and muttered. Why did Jesus mix with tax collectors and other bad people? "I have come to help the people who need me most," said Jesus.

262

Happy people

Matthew 5:1-12

Wherever Jesus went, people followed him. So he sat down to teach them. "God will bless you if you know you need his help. God will comfort you if you are sad. God will satisfy you if you long for good things and he will be kind to you if you are kind to others."

263

Be kind to everyone

Matthew 5:43-44

"Love other people. Forgive them if they hurt you. Treat them the way you yourself would like to be treated," said Jesus. "But love your enemies too and pray for them. Otherwise the people who love God are no different from everyone else. Be perfect, just like God himself."

264

How to pray

Matthew 6:5-8

"Talk to God in secret, as if you are talking to a father who loves you and cares about you," said Jesus. "Don't pray just so that other people will be impressed. Tell God that you love him. Tell him what worries you. Be honest. God will answer. He knows what you need."

265

The Lord's prayer

Matthew 6:9-13

"If you don't know how to start praying, try this, 'Our Father in heaven, your name is holy. May peace and justice and all good things happen here just as they do in heaven. Give us what we need to eat today. Forgive us when we hurt others and help us to forgive people who hurt us.'"

266

Don't worry!

Matthew 6:25-34

"Do you ever worry?" asked Jesus. "Sparrows don't worry about how they'll find food. The flowers don't worry about the clothes they wear. God feeds the sparrows and makes the flowers beautiful. Trust God and put him first and he will give you everything else you need."

267

The wise man listens

Luke 6:46-48

Many people heard what Jesus taught. But Jesus said it wasn't enough just to listen and agree. "The person who acts on my words and does what is right is like someone who builds their house on a rock. When the stormy times come, the house will be safe and strong."

268

The foolish man closes his ears

Luke 6:49

"But," said Jesus, "the person who ignores these words is like someone who builds their house on the sand. When the stormy times come, the walls fall down and the roof falls in. Their house and all they have worked for is washed away. Be wise. Listen and do what is right."

269

The centurion's servant

Matthew 8:5-9

When Jesus came to Capernaum, a Roman centurion asked for his help. "My servant is suffering in great pain," the man said. "But I know you can heal him. I don't deserve you to come into my house. Just say that he is healed and I know that he will be."

270

The servant is healed

Matthew 8:10-13

Jesus was surprised. "I have never seen such faith before, not even among Abraham's descendants!" Jesus said. "God welcomes people everywhere to believe and you clearly trust God. Go home now. Your servant is well again." When the man returned to his house, his servant had been healed.

271
The widow's son

Luke 7:11-15

When Jesus and his friends visited Nain, they saw the body of a young man being carried away to be buried. His mother, a widow, was weeping for her only son. Jesus saw how sad she was. He touched the man, and immediately he was restored to life. The woman was overjoyed.

272

Treasure in the field

Matthew 13:44

Jesus often told stories to help people understand what he was saying. "God's kingdom is like buried treasure in a field," Jesus said once. "When a man found this treasure, he sold everything he had to buy the field because the treasure was so precious. Follow God's way. It's the best thing you will ever do."

273
The storm on the lake

Luke 8:22-23

Jesus was very tired. He got into a boat with his disciples and they sailed to the other side of Lake Galilee. But soon Jesus fell asleep. Then the sky changed color and the gentle breeze became a wind that tossed the boat high on the rough waves. Even the fishermen were afraid!

274

Jesus calms the storm

Luke 8:24-25

"Master! Wake up! We're going to drown!" the disciples cried out. Jesus stood up. He told the wind to stop blowing. He told the waves to be calm. The boat gently drifted on the water once more. "Didn't you trust me?" Jesus asked the disciples. The disciples were amazed. How did Jesus do that?

275
Jairus' little girl

Luke 8:40-42

One day a man called Jairus came to ask Jesus for help. "Please come to my house!" he begged. "My only daughter is dying. She's only twelve years old!" Crowds of people had come to see Jesus and were all around him. But Jesus made his way through the people, following Jairus.

276

The woman in the crowd

Luke 8:43-48

A woman in the crowd had been ill for twelve years. She didn't want to make a fuss but she needed Jesus' help too. If only she could touch the hem of his clothes... Suddenly Jesus stopped. "Who touched me?" he asked. Then he smiled at the woman. "It's OK," said Jesus. "Your faith has healed you."

277

Jairus' daughter

Luke 9:49-56

But it was too late for Jairus' daughter. A messenger came to say that she had died. "Only believe and she will be well," Jesus told Jairus. Jesus sent away all the weeping women and went into the house. "Get up, little girl," he said. Jairus' daughter sat up. Jesus had healed her!

278
Loaves and fishes

Luke 9:12-15

One day Jesus
talked to a crowd
of over 5,000 people!
But as it grew late
in the day, Jesus was
concerned that the people would
be hungry. "We must find food
for everyone here," Jesus told
his disciples. "But we only
have five pieces of bread
and two fishes," they said.

279

Baskets of leftovers

Luke 9:16-17

The disciples told the people to sit down while Jesus thanked God for the bread and the fish. Jesus broke them into pieces and gave them to the disciples to share among the people. Everyone shared until they had eaten enough. There were even twelve baskets of leftovers! It was a miracle!

280

Jesus walks on water

Matthew 14:22-26

Later that evening, Jesus asked the disciples to row across the lake while he stayed behind. He wanted to be alone to pray for a while. The boat was a long way from the shore when suddenly the men saw someone coming toward them, walking on the water! "Don't be afraid," Jesus shouted. "It's only me."

281

Peter is afraid

Matthew 14:27-31

Peter replied, "Lord, if it's really you, let me come to you on the water." Peter got out of the boat and started to walk toward Jesus. But suddenly the wind blew around him and he started to sink. Jesus took his hand and helped him back in the boat. "Why were you afraid?" Jesus asked.

282

Jesus heals a deaf man

Mark 7:32-37

As Jesus visited the places all around Lake Galilee, a man was brought to him who could not hear and who could hardly speak at all. Jesus took the man away from the crowd. He touched his ears and tongue and healed him. The people were overjoyed when the man started to speak to them!

The story of the good Samaritan

Luke 10:30-32

Jesus once told a story to show people what loving God really meant. "A man was traveling from Jerusalem to Jericho when he was attacked by robbers. A priest and a Levite passed him as he lay wounded on the road – but neither man stopped to help him."

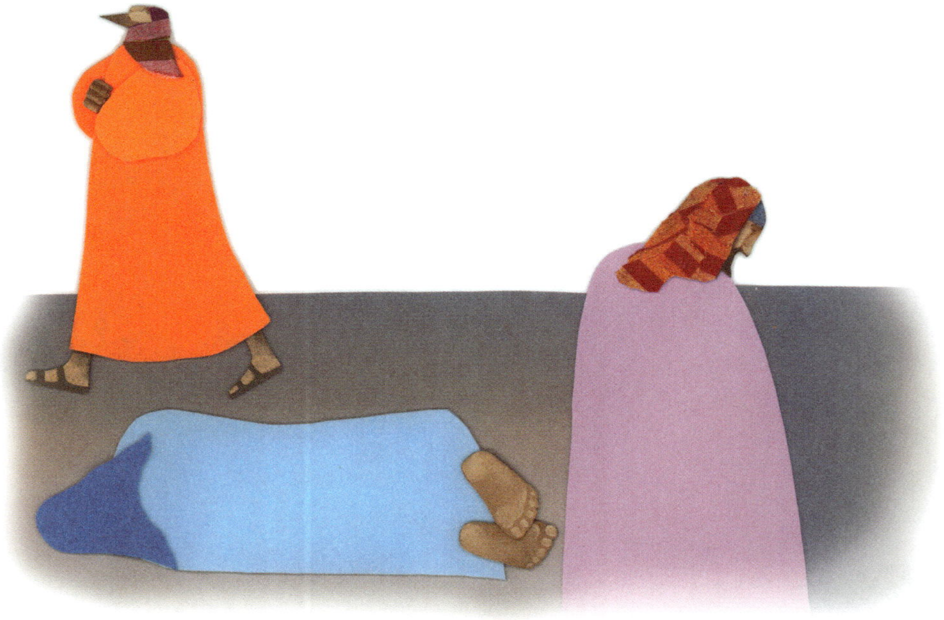

284

Loving your neighbor

Luke 10:33-37

"Then a Samaritan came along the road. Everyone knows that Israelites and Samaritans are not friends. But the Samaritan stopped and bandaged the man's wounds. He took him to an inn and paid for the man to be looked after till he was well. This is what it means to love your neighbor," said Jesus.

285

The good shepherd

John 10:11-15

The land that Jesus lived in had many sheep on the hillsides. They may have looked alike to a stranger. But the shepherds knew their sheep and the sheep knew the shepherd's voice. "You are like my sheep," said Jesus. "I am the Good Shepherd, and I would even die to take care of my sheep."

286

The story of the lost sheep

Luke 15:3-7

"Imagine you own a hundred sheep," said Jesus. "One day you find that there are only 99. You search everywhere for that little lost sheep. You cannot rest till you carry him home again on your shoulders! God's love is like that. He cares about everyone, especially the one that is lost and alone."

287

The story of the lost son

Luke 15:11-19

"God loves you all," said Jesus. "Even when you make mistakes he is ready to forgive you – like the father in this story. A man had two sons. One day the younger son asked for his share of his father's money. He left home and had a great time – until there was no money left."

288

The story of the loving father

Luke 15:20-32

"Soon the boy was starving. He went home, hungry and dirty and dressed in rags. 'Father,' the boy said, 'I've been so silly and I am really sorry...' But instead of being angry, the father hugged his lost son. 'Let's celebrate!' he said. 'I have been waiting for you. My son was lost, but now he's found!'"

289

Treasure on earth

Luke 12:16-19

Jesus told another story about money and possessions. "Try not to be greedy," Jesus said. "Life is more important than the things money can buy. Listen! Once there was a farmer who had a very good harvest. He pulled down the barns he had and built much bigger barns to store all his crops."

290

Treasure in heaven

Luke 12:20-20, 33-34

"The man planned to relax and enjoy the good things he had stored up for himself. But that night, he died. What good were his riches to him now? So," said Jesus, "share what you have, and store up treasure in heaven, where moths cannot eat it and robbers cannot steal it."

291

Jesus heals ten lepers

Luke 17:11-14

Ten men stood huddled together, waiting for Jesus at the edge of a village. Their clothes were ragged and they were covered in bandages. Jesus knew they had a skin disease called leprosy. They were not allowed to live with their families in case they became ill too. "Help us, Lord!" they cried. "Go home," said Jesus. "I have healed you."

292

The man who said "Thank you!"

Luke 17:14-19

The men laughed and danced and showed each other their smooth, healthy skin. But one man ran after Jesus. "Thank you, Lord, for making me well!" he said. Jesus smiled at the man. "Your faith has healed you," he said. But Jesus looked sadly into the distance at the other nine.

293

Lazarus and his sisters

John 11: 1-17

Jesus was very good friends with a man named Lazarus and his sisters, Mary and Martha. One day, someone came to tell him that Lazarus was very ill. Jesus knew that he could help his friend, but he did not go to him straight away. Instead Jesus stayed teaching the people where he was, traveling a few days later.

294

The death of Lazarus

John 11:18-33

Martha met Jesus on the road to their house and told him that Lazarus had died and been buried four days before. "Lord, if you had been here, I know my brother would still be alive," she said. Her eyes were wet with tears. "But I know you are God's son. God will give you whatever you ask."

295

Jesus makes Lazarus live!

John 11:34-46

Mary and the rest of the family came with them to the place where Lazarus had been buried. Jesus was so sad that he cried for his friend. But then he prayed, "Father, now show everyone that you have sent me here." Jesus turned and said, "Lazarus! Come out!" And Lazarus walked out from the tomb – alive!

296

Jesus blesses children

Mark 10:13-16

Crowds of people gathered wherever Jesus went. Mothers brought their children to be blessed by him. Jesus always had time for them. He laughed with the children and hugged them. "My Kingdom is made up of people like these children," Jesus said. "They are ready to love and trust God with all their hearts."

297

The rich man

Mark 10:17-25

A rich young man once asked Jesus, "What do I have to do to live in heaven?" Jesus knew the man had a good heart, but there was one thing wrong. "Love God more than you love your money," Jesus answered. "Give it away to the poor." The man was very sad. He knew that he could not do it.

298

The blind beggar

Luke 18:35-39

Jesus was traveling to Jericho and the streets were lined with people. "What's all the noise about?" a blind beggar asked. Someone told him that Jesus was passing by. The blind man had heard all about Jesus. Perhaps Jesus would help him. "Jesus, Son of David, have mercy on me!" he shouted.

299
The blind man sees!

Luke 18:35-43

"Be quiet!" people shouted back. "Jesus is busy!" But the blind beggar kept trying to get Jesus' attention. Jesus stopped. "What do you want me to do for you?" he asked. "I want to see!" the blind man said. "Your faith has made you well," Jesus replied. "Go now: you can see!"

300

The little tax collector

Luke 19:1-4

Elbow to elbow, the streets were packed as Jesus went through Jericho. And no one was going to make room for Zacchaeus, the rich tax collector. He was a cheat! Zacchaeus was very short, so he climbed up a fig tree to see Jesus as he passed. But Jesus stopped right under the tree.

301

Zacchaeus meets Jesus

Luke 19:5-10

"Zacchaeus, I'd like to visit your house today," Jesus said. All the people were shocked. But Zacchaeus changed when he met Jesus. "I'm going to give half my money to the poor and stop being a cheat," he said. And Jesus told everyone, "I came to find people, like Zacchaeus, who need God's help."

302

People who are kind

Matthew 25:31-34

"One day God will judge everyone according to how they have lived," Jesus told his disciples. "'You have done well,' he will say to some. 'When I was hungry, you gave me food. When I needed clothes, you shared yours with me. When I was in prison or in hospital, you visited me.'"

303

People who are selfish

Matthew 25:35-46

"God will say to the others, 'Go away from me! You would not help when I was cold and hungry, in prison or in hospital.' They will ask, 'But when did we do these things?' God's answer will be, 'Whenever you saw someone who needed help and you refused to give it, you were refusing to help me.'"

304

Mary anoints Jesus

John 12:1-8

Jesus went to visit his friends, Lazarus, Martha and Mary. When they sat down to eat, Mary poured some expensive perfume on Jesus' feet. Then she dried his feet with her long hair. "What a waste!" said Judas. "No," replied Jesus. "I will not be here much longer. What Mary has done is kind and caring."

305

Jesus the King

John 12:12-19

Jesus decided to ride into Jerusalem for the Passover feast, riding on a donkey. Long ago, a prophet wrote that their king would ride a donkey, not a war horse. So when people saw him coming, they waved branches from palm trees. "God bless, Jesus," they shouted and cheered! "Jesus is our king!"

306

A place to pray

Mark 11:15-18

When Jesus came to the temple, he saw many people selling animals for offerings. He saw money-changers cheating the visitors. Crash! Bang! Jesus turned over their tables. "God's house is a place for kindness and caring, and for people to pray," Jesus said. "It's not a place for cheating and stealing!"

307

A woman who loved God

Mark 12:41-44

Clink. Clink. A poor widow came to give two copper coins for God's work. "Look," Jesus said to his disciples. "This woman has given more than all the rich people here. Everyone else gave what they had left over when they had spent lots of money on themselves. She gave God everything that she had."

308

Plots against Jesus

Matthew 26:3-5

"We have to get rid of Jesus!" the priests and religious leaders said. "But all the people love him! We must do it secretly." Jesus knew about their plots and plans. "The Passover feast will soon be here," Jesus told his disciples. "It will not be long until they take me away and crucify me."

309

Show that you love each other

John 13:5-20

Jesus met all his disciples in an upstairs room. Before they ate together, Jesus filled a basin with water. "I am going to wash your feet," he told them. "Follow my example. Show that you care about each other by doing things like this. Show the world that you love me by loving each other."

Who will betray Jesus?

John 13:21-25

Jesus was surrounded by his twelve disciples for the last time. "You are all my friends. But I know that one of you will betray me." The disciples could not believe it! They had all seen the wonderful things he did. "Who is it, Lord?" they asked. Jesus wouldn't tell them. But Judas felt uncomfortable.

311

Who will deny Jesus?

John 13:31-38

"I want you to love each another just as I have loved you," Jesus said. Peter jumped up. "Surely you know that I would do anything for you, Lord!" Jesus smiled sadly back at Peter. "Oh, Peter. Before the cock crows at dawn tomorrow, you will have said three times that you do not even know me."

312
Judas creeps away

John 13:26-31

Jesus turned to Judas and said, "Do what you have to do now, but go quickly." The other disciples thought that Judas was going to give money to the poor. Thirty silver coins jingled in his pocket. It was not for the poor – it was the money Judas had been given to take the religious leaders to Jesus.

313

A house with many rooms

John 14:1-6

"Soon I will go to my father's house where there are many rooms, and I will make a place ready for you," Jesus said. "How will we get there, Lord?" Thomas asked. "I am the way, the truth, and the life. I am the bridge between you and God," Jesus answered.

314

The last supper

Mark 14:22-25

This would be the last meal Jesus ate with his disciples before his death. He broke some bread. "Eat this," he said. "This is my body which is broken for you." Then Jesus took a cup of wine and said, "Drink this. This is my blood which will be given for you."

315

Praying in the garden

Matthew 26:36-38

After supper, Jesus and his friends went to a garden called Gethsemane. Silver grey olive trees lit by the full moon surrounded them. Jesus said to Peter, John and James, "I feel very sad and lonely. Please stay close by and pray with me." Then Jesus went a little further and prayed to God.

316

Jesus is alone

Matthew 26:39

"Father God," Jesus prayed. "I know that there is much sadness and suffering to come. I know that soon I must die. But please, if there is any other way to save the people that you love, then help me now. If not, then I want to do whatever you want. Please help me to do it bravely."

317

Sleeping friends

Matthew 26:40-46

After a while, Jesus walked back to see his friends. But all the disciples – even Peter, John and James - had fallen asleep while Jesus was praying! Jesus woke them and asked them again to watch and pray for him. Then he went to pray by himself again. But his friends just couldn't stay awake.

318

Judas leads the armed guards

Matthew 26:47-56

Suddenly it was too late. "The time has come for me to be taken prisoner," Jesus said. In the quiet garden, they could hear men approaching. Here was Judas coming to kiss him. But was Judas really his friend? He was leading lots of armed guards! The kiss was a signal. Now the guards knew which man to arrest.

319

Jesus is a prisoner!

Mark 14:46-50

The men surrounded Jesus and arrested him. "Why do you need swords and clubs?" asked Jesus. "Every day I have been in the temple or with the people. You didn't arrest me then!" The disciples were terrified! They didn't know what to do. They ran away and left their friend, alone with the armed men.

320
"Are you the Son of God?"

Matthew 26:57-68

The guards marched Jesus away to the house of Caiaphas, the high priest. The religious leaders had gathered to put Jesus on trial. "Tell us whether you are the Christ, the Son of God," they demanded. Jesus simply said, "You have said it yourself." Caiaphas was very angry! How could this man claim to be God?

321

Peter is ashamed

Matthew 26:69-75

Peter and John were afraid. They didn't want to be seen. But they wanted to know where Jesus was. A servant girl said to Peter, "Aren't you a friend of that man?" Then a man said the same. Someone else said he had the same accent as Jesus. Three times Peter said no! Then he heard the cock crow... It was dawn.

322

Pontius Pilate

Matthew 27:11-22

Only Pontius Pilate, the Roman governor, could decide if someone should die. The religious leaders brought Jesus to him. "This man is a troublemaker!" they said. Pilate could tell Jesus was innocent. But he didn't want more trouble. What should he do? Outside, a bloodthirsty crowd was shouting, "Crucify him! Crucify him!"

323
Pilate frees a murderer

Matthew 27:22-26

The angry crowd looked up at Pontius Pilate. He knew Jesus had done nothing wrong, but he was afraid. "I can set a prisoner free as it is almost Passover," he said. "Barabbas, the murderer? Or the man you call your King - Jesus from Nazareth?" "Free Barabbas!" they shouted. "Crucify Jesus!"

324

The crown of thorns

Matthew 27:27-32

It was a Friday morning when the Roman soldiers took Jesus away. They dressed him in a scarlet robe and put a stick in his hand. "You're supposed to be a king, aren't you?" they said, laughing. "You need a crown!" The soldiers beat him and pushed a crown of sharp thorns on to his head.

325

Jesus carries his cross

Mark 15:20-22

The soldiers led Jesus away to the place of crucifixion. Prisoners had to carry the heavy piece of wood that would become part of the cross they would die on. But Jesus, tired and weak from the beating, kept stumbling. The soldiers made a man named Simon carry the wood the rest of the way.

326
A cross between two thieves

Luke 23: 32-43

As the soldiers nailed Jesus to his cross, he said, "Forgive them, Father!" Then Jesus was crucified between two thieves. One shouted, "You saved other people: save yourself!" But the other said, "Leave him alone! He does not deserve punishment, as we do! Please, Jesus, remember me." Jesus answered, "Today you will be with me in heaven."

327

Jesus looks after his mother

John 19:26-27

Hours passed while Jesus was on the cross. Jesus saw his mother and his friend John standing nearby, weeping. "Mother!" Jesus said. "Treat John as your son now." Then he looked at John and said, "Look after Mary as your own mother." John comforted Mary as she stood and waited for her son to die.

328

Jesus dies on the cross

Matthew 27:50-54

It was still daytime when the sky went dark. Jesus was alone. He thought that God, his Father, had deserted him. He knew that he was dying instead of all the people in the world who had ever sinned and who would ever sin in the future. He cried out in a loud voice once more. Then Jesus died.

329

On Friday evening

Mark 15:42-46

There was a rich man called Joseph of Arimathea who had been one of Jesus' friends. He went to Pilate and asked if he could take down Jesus' body from the cross and bury him in his own tomb before the Sabbath day. The soldiers put a sword in his side to make sure Jesus was dead.

330

Buried in a cave

John 19:38-42

Joseph and another friend, Nicodemus, took Jesus' body and placed it in a tomb which was in a garden near the cross. They wound a clean linen sheet around his body with special spices. Then they rolled a large stone against the entrance to close it tightly.

331

The empty tomb

John 19:42–20:1

The next day was the Sabbath, a special day of rest. So it was early on Sunday morning, while it was still dark, that Mary Magdalene came to visit the place where she had seen Jesus buried. But the large stone had been rolled away. When she peeped inside, the tomb was empty!

332

Jesus is alive!

John 20:1-18

Mary went to tell Peter and John and they ran to the tomb to see for themselves. What could this mean? Then they left Mary weeping in the garden. But someone else came and comforted her. "Mary," a voice spoke kindly. Mary knew that voice. It was Jesus! He was not dead any more. Jesus was alive!

333

The man who blessed the bread

Luke 24:13-35

Cleopas and a friend were walking to Emmaus, talking about the terrible things that had happened to Jesus that week. Someone joined them as they walked and they invited him to eat with them. When the man broke the bread and asked God to bless it – they saw that it was Jesus!

334
Inside a locked room

John 20:19-23

That same day, some of the disciples were together in a room. The doors were locked. They were very sad because Jesus had died. They were also afraid. Suddenly, everything changed. They were no longer alone. Jesus was there in the room with them! "You're alive!" they shouted. "You have risen from the dead!"

335
Thomas doubts

John 20:24-29

Thomas had not been with the other disciples when Jesus had come to them. Now he could not believe that Jesus was alive. "I must see him with my own eyes," he said. Eight days later, Jesus appeared again. "Look at the nail marks Thomas," Jesus said. Thomas fell to his knees. It really was Jesus!

336

Night fishing on Lake Galilee

John 21:1-6

"Let's go fishing," Peter said to his friends one evening. After many hours on Lake Galilee, they hadn't caught anything. It was nearly dawn when a man called to them from the shore. "Throw your net on the right side of the boat!" When Peter did, the net was filled with fish!

337
Breakfast with Jesus

John 21:7-11

Splash! Peter jumped into the water and swam to shore. He knew the man must be Jesus! There was a warm fire and bread waiting for them. "Bring some of the fish you caught," Jesus said. "Let's have breakfast." The disciples brought in the heavy net. They had caught 153 fish!

338

Peter is forgiven

John 21:15-17

Jesus knew that Peter was still sad.
Jesus walked along the shore with him.
He asked him the same question three times,
just as Peter had denied him three times.
"Peter, do you love me?" he asked. "Yes, I do, Lord!"
"I have a special job for you," Jesus said.
"I want you to look after my followers."

339

Jesus returns to heaven

Acts 1:1-11

"It's time for me to return to God, my Father," Jesus told his friends. "I will come back one day. But now you must wait for the Holy Spirit to come. Then it will be as if I were always there to help you." Jesus then left his friends and returned to heaven.

340

Waiting in Jerusalem

Acts 1:12-26

About 120 people gathered together in Jerusalem. All were friends or disciples of Jesus. "We need someone to take Judas' place," said Peter. "We must pray that God will help us choose the right person." Then Matthias, who had been with them since the day Jesus was baptized by John, became the twelfth disciple.

341

The Holy Spirit comes

Acts 2:1-4

Many people from all over the world came to Jerusalem to celebrate the harvest at the feast of Pentecost. All Jesus' friends were together when whoosh! - a sound like a rushing wind filled the house. The Holy Spirit came to the disciples giving them strength to do the good things that Jesus wanted them to do.

342

Peter talks about Jesus

Acts 2:14-36

The Holy Spirit helped the disciples to talk about Jesus in many different languages. Peter spoke to the crowd that had gathered. "You crucified Jesus – but God gave him new life! Now believe that Jesus is the Son of God and he will forgive you." That day about 3000 people became Christians.

343

The man at the Beautiful Gate

Acts 3:1-10

A man sat by one of the temple gates begging day after day because he could not walk. "I don't have any silver or gold," Peter said, "but with Jesus' help, I can help you to walk." Then the man was healed! He jumped up and down with joy, thanking God for healing him.

344
Peter's message

Acts 4:1-4

Everyone in the temple courtyard was amazed at what had happened. "Why are you surprised?" asked Peter. "You allowed Pilate to crucify Jesus. But God raised Jesus to new life and by the same power, this man can now walk!" The temple guards didn't like this at all. They grabbed Peter and John and threw them into prison.

345

Prisoners for God

Acts 4:5-18

Peter and John were questioned the next morning. "How did you heal this man?" The Holy Spirit helped Peter to answer, just as Jesus had promised. "Jesus healed him. And only Jesus can heal and forgive and save any of us. You have seen this miracle for yourselves. We cannot help tell everyone about Jesus!"

346
Peter and John are free

Acts 4:4, 21-35

There were now about 5000 believers in Jerusalem, sharing with each other everything they owned, living the way that Jesus had taught them. "Help us not to be afraid as we tell people about you, Lord," they prayed. "Let people see miracles and know that you are the true and living God."

347

The first Christian martyr

Acts 6:1 – 7:60

The twelve disciples chose seven men to help them look after people who were ill or poor. Stephen was one of them. God blessed him so that he was able to heal many people and speak bravely about Jesus. The temple elders hated him. They arranged for him to be stoned to death.

348

A Pharisee named Saul

Acts 8:1, 9:1-2

Saul believed in God. He was sure that the Christians were wrong about Jesus and hated all that they said and did. So when Stephen was killed, Saul looked on, pleased at what had happened. Then he went from house to house, looking for all the believers and throwing them into prison.

349

The man in the chariot

Acts 8:26-30

The new Christians had asked for God's help. Now they needed it more than ever. Those who were not imprisoned left Jerusalem, but wherever they went, they told people about Jesus. On the road to Gaza, Philip met an important man from Ethiopia reading aloud from one of the prophecies about Jesus.

350

Philip baptizes the Ethiopian

Acts 8:30-38

"Do you understand what you are reading," Philip asked. "No. Please help me," the man replied. So Philip told him that God had sent Jesus, his son, to die on a cross. Anyone who trusted him could be forgiven for all the wrong things they had done. The man did trust Jesus. He asked Philip to baptize him!

351

Jesus talks to Saul

Acts 9:3-6

Saul was on his way to Damascus when suddenly, he was blinded by a light from heaven. "Saul, why are you persecuting me?" "Who are you?" asked Saul, who couldn't see who was speaking. "I am Jesus," came the answer. "Listen to me from now on. I have an important job for you to do."

352

Cornelius sees an angel

Acts 10:1-8

A Roman soldier named Cornelius had learned about God while working in Israel. Cornelius and his family loved God and prayed often. So when an angel appeared one day with a message for him, he listened. "God has heard your prayers," said the angel. "Find Peter and he will teach you more."

353

A vision on the rooftop

Acts 10:9-16

Meanwhile, Peter was resting on the roof of a house. As he fell asleep, he dreamed that God was offering him all kinds of birds and animals to eat, including those normally forbidden. "But these animals aren't clean, Lord," Peter said. God replied, "Once that was true, but now I have made them clean and holy."

354
Peter meets Cornelius

Acts 10:24-33

The angel had told Cornelius to find Peter. So Cornelius invited him to his house. When Peter met the soldier, he understood his strange dreams. Peter and his friends had always believed that they were God's holy chosen people. But Jesus had come to make everyone welcome in God's kingdom – even Roman soldiers.

355

Passover in prison

Acts 12:1-6

Herod Agrippa was now king in Judea. He had James, John's brother, put to death. Then he put Peter in prison. He planned to give him a public trial before killing him too! So Peter spent Passover in chains. There was a guard on either side of him and two more soldiers guarding the door!

356

People pray for Peter

Acts 12:5-6

But Peter was not alone. His friends were praying for him. God was caring for him. Mary, the mother of John Mark, invited many of Jesus' followers to her house. They prayed for their friend into the late hours of the night. God answered their prayers. He sent an angel to rescue Peter!

357

A knocking at the door

Acts 12:7-11

"Bang! Bang!" Rhoda went to answer the door. "It's Peter!" she told everyone. "He's free!" No one would believe her – until Peter was there with them in the room. "An angel came to my prison cell," he told his friends. "The chains fell off my wrists and the city gates opened by themselves! I thought I was dreaming – but God has set me free!"

358
Paul tells people about Jesus

Acts 16:9-15

Remember Saul, the man who hated Christians? The Christians called him Paul. Now he had met Jesus for himself he was a changed man. And he was so happy to know Jesus that he told everyone he knew about him. A businesswoman named Lydia heard Paul preaching in a place called Philippi and asked to be baptized.

359

Paul in trouble!

Acts 16:16-26

In Macedonia, a slave girl made her masters rich by telling fortunes. Paul set her free of the evil spirit inside her – but then she could no longer see the future. Her masters were so angry, Paul was thrown into prison. Paul didn't care. He praised God there just as he did out of prison.

360
A miracle in the prison cell

Acts 16:27-40

Suddenly there was an earthquake and the chains fell off Paul's hands. The prison guard was so sure Paul would escape, he drew his sword to kill himself. "Stop!" Paul shouted. "But how can I be saved?" said the guard. "Trust Jesus and be baptized!" Paul answered. So the guard and all his family became Christians that day.

361

Paul's journeys

Acts 13 - 20

Paul was released from prison. He spent many years traveling. He told people that God loved them so much that he had sent Jesus to die on a cross for them. Everywhere Paul went, people believed his message and wanted to be baptized. New Christian churches were started in many different countries.

362

Paul's sufferings

Acts 21:15-26:32

Paul had no real home. Sometimes people threw stones at him and drove him away. He suffered many bad things as he traveled from country to country. When he went home to Jerusalem, he was arrested and imprisoned for years. As he was a Roman citizen, Paul asked to see the emperor in Rome.

363

The violent storm

Acts 27:1-20

Luke, the doctor, traveled with him on the ship that took him to Rome. At first the sea was calm but soon, a violent wind tossed the ship around. Waves lashed at the deck and no sun, moon or stars could be seen. The sailors were terrified but Paul knew that God would not let them die.

364

A shipwreck near Malta

Acts 27:21-28:1

Eventually they saw land. But the ship got stuck on a sand bank and part of it broke up. They reached the shore by swimming or clinging to parts of the broken ship. All 276 people on the boat landed safely and were looked after by the people of Malta. Even there Paul prayed for people and healed them.

365

Letters from Rome

Acts 28:11-31

When they finally reached Rome, Paul was allowed to stay in a house with a soldier to guard him. He spent the rest of his life writing letters to Christians in all the countries he had visited, encouraging them to follow Jesus.

More than two thousand years later,
new Christians are still being baptized
in every corner of the world.

AN ANNO DOMINI BOOK

Publishing Director: Annette Reynolds
Art Director: Gerald Rogers
Pre-production Manager: Krystyna Kowalska Hewitt
Production Manager: John Laister

First US edition 2013

US and Canadian distribution
Book Depot
67 Front Street North
Thorold, Ontario, L2V 1X3
Canada
www.bookdepot.com

Printed and bound in Singapore